CU01011205

Dear Mark and Sarah...

22 Letters dealing with
Ministry to Children
Depression
Curses
Dreams etc.

Beryl E. Burgess

New Wine Press

New Wine Press
PO Box 17
Chichester, PO20 6YB
England

The author would like to acknowledge the support The Order of
St. Luke the Physician in New Zealand, has given her in her ministry.

ISBN: 1 874367 81

Typeset by CRB Associates, Reepham, Norfolk
Printed in England by Clays Ltd, St Ives plc.

Foreword

I have great pleasure in recommending this book particularly for all those who are concerned with the raising, caring or praying for children in any way. Having spent a number of years as a primary schoolteacher as well as teaching Seminars concerned with 'Healing and Praying for your Children', I have found Beryl Burgess's book invaluable. Her wisdom and insight, especially in the area of praying for children through intercession, has deep lessons to teach us all.

Beryl has grasped and based her work on a very important belief, which is that God hears and heeds the cry of the heart – whether that is of a parent, friend, grandparent, teacher or whomever – for the needs of the hurting and wounded.

She has also based her work on the truth that we can intercede for people without them being present. This may be vitally important in some instances, as she demonstrates in her book.

I am delighted that this book is being reprinted and suggest that there should be a copy on every church bookshelf, as well as in the lounge of every parent.

Ruth Hawkey
May 1998

PART ONE

Letter 1

Dear Mark and Sarah

I am still excited about the way we met each other again after so long. It was wonderful to see you both but a pity we did not have more time together. I know you have a great deal to tell me and I, of course, also have much to share with you.

Because we are far apart and you are so deeply interested in the way my life and ministry have developed, I have decided to write you a letter every few weeks to condense if I can, the events and experiences of the past few years.

I know that you believe as I do, that God leads each of us in his or her own special way and not one of us needs to follow blindly the way that another has walked. It is good however, to share what we have learned and if this sharing leads to something valuable, so much the better. I know how much you want to care for, and minister to, the people around you and it is good to grow together in love.

To begin with, do you remember how we all struggled together concerning the healing ministry of the Church and how we watched the climate of thinking slowly emerge from the ice age? We read many fine books and and experimented a great deal with healing through prayer. They were great days. Since then much more literature has become available and we are better informed about, and more willing to use, the services available through praying friends, family and clergy. It has been wonderful to be part of it all.

We have learned about the power of God – in Jesus' name – to heal physical ills, and have puzzled along with many others, as to why it doesn't always seem to work that way. There are still so many unsolved mysteries. We have also learned of the same power to heal the sicknesses of the spirit and have marvelled at the transformation we have seen coming about in people's lives before our very eyes. It is indeed a stark necessity for the 'inside person' to be healed of his or her painful memories. Often a physical condition is cured or vastly improved, when the inner hurts and fears are healed. Everyone gathers some of these hurts and fears in the process of learning to live in this imperfect world. I spent five years as a Lay Pastor in a busy suburban church and they were truly wonderful years, but in the course of my work in that time, one thing became as obvious as the proverbial sore toe – the plight of the children.

One does not have to look far these days to find sick children, bewildered children, grieving children, rebellious children, children with physical problems, mental problems and problems which plainly arise from incidents in the past. Sometimes of course, there have been problem parents too, but it is the children that I really want to talk about.

You will have read or heard about the healing of memories in adults and of how some damaging, fear producing incidents of situations occurring in childhood can cause a grown person to be deprived of a full life in the present. You will have met some folks with such fears. There are fears of doctors, dentists, water, dogs, spiders, the dark, open spaces, closed spaces, heights, depths. Fears of being rejected or ridiculed, of being a failure – or a success – fears of loneliness, illness, bereavement. One may fear having no home, no job, no security, no love, no appreciation. The list is endless. So often, after prayers for the healing of the wounds of the spirit, and an act of forgiveness towards the people or incidents involved in the distress, there has been great freedom from the hurts and inhibitions of the past. This is wonderful, but these folk were adult. What of the children and young people?

Many who crossed my path were at that very moment, living through incidents and struggling with situations which clearly would need to be dealt with later in their lives. My spirit strove with the problem. Why wait? Was there not something that could be done in the here and now? Many parents were only too pleased to try anything – yet what did one tell them to try? One could say tell them to pray, but not how to pray.

If one believes with all one's heart and soul that Jesus is the Lord of time, then surely it follows that if He can heal and restore damage which is happening now then He can also heal and restore damage which occurred in the past. This is the principle in which all healing of the memories is based. You could call it 'Itemised Intercession'. It didn't seem to be enough to simply 'commit' the person into God's hands with a prayer to bless them. If our faith was going to be used to help others, then we would have to 'bite off the right-sized lumps' of the problem – 'lumps' that we could believe for and 'see' changed in our mind's eye.

If rebellious Janey – who was anti-work, anti-study, anti-sport, anti-father, anti-stepmother, anti-people in general – was to be healed, it appeared that one had to retrace the steps of the years back to a time when a little girl of seven years old had lost her mother – to when that little girl, bereft and lonely, figuratively shook her fist at the world and said in her innermost being, 'life has dealt me a dirty deal! I hate life! I hate people! I hate everything!'

One had to pray in faith that the loving arms of Jesus would surround and comfort that child, at that time. One had to 'see' it happening in one's mind's eye and watch with thanksgiving for the improvement in her life and conduct which that comfort could be expected to bring about.

Letter 1

When a grown person is in need nearly always they are aware of it and often try to take steps to have the situation remedied and the need met. One can usually get at least a degree of cooperation from them, no matter how ill or depressed they are. The children however, are often unaware of their deep needs. They feel unhappy, but they don't know why. Sometimes they don't even remember ever feeling any different, or if they do remember, they cannot speak of it. Perhaps it would hurt too much, or perhaps their vocabularies are limited. They may even lack the necessary words to verbalise their feelings. The 'needs' in such cases are often noticed by parents, other family members, teachers or other children.

To reduce the results of many months of experimental intercession into a few words, I developed a 'technique' or a 'system' of praying through a child's life. I would begin at the moment of conception, continue through the birth process, then on to babyhood, to the toddler stage and to school days, until I arrived at the age which I now knew the child to be. 'But,' you will ask, 'how did you know what to pray for?' It is surprising how much information parents and friends give, if only one will listen!

Certain things apply to all children but in each particular case one must ask God, the Holy Spirit, to bring to mind those things which need to be dealt with in this particular instance. Sometimes there are reports of observed behaviour. Other times, one's own remembered experiences come to mind. Having asked God to guide us, how often, when we remember an incident in our own lives, do we dismiss it and say, 'But that couldn't have happened to anyone else.' Who says not? Why not act on it? Surely it is better to cover too much than too little.

When one embarks on this kind of intercession, various faults and shortcomings begin to emerge much more clearly in one's own life. I found myself praying for wisdom, for discernment, for the ability to concentrate for longer periods of time and for the capacity to sort out the important from the unimportant. I became aware of a tendency to let my own thoughts run on at a purely human level, and of a failure to hear the voice of God clearly, mainly because of insufficient discipline concerning reading and prayer time. All these things had to be remedied and it was often a slow and painful process. The concentration problem is often solved, to some extent, by the simple expedient of asking a friend to join in, and by always praying aloud.

I have several wonderful friends who work with me. The first person may pray about, say, the period of the child's life ranging from the time of conception to three years, then the other one will continue with the period from three to six years, then the first person will take from six to nine years and so on, until the child's present age is reached. If the child is very small, the partners can alternate with shorter periods of time. Each person must find the method which suits them best. This is simply what happened with me.

I have been really grateful at times for a certain streak of dogged tenacity, which is not always a reason for gratitude! It seems that the word 'faith', as I understand it, carries with it a certain connotation of patient persistence. If we pray and there appears to be little or no improvement, then we don't give up. Perhaps we make certain adjustments and try again. Often the positive answers seem to depend on learning how to make the right requests.

If I were in trouble or ill, I wouldn't want anyone to give up on me. This came to me one day while I was waiting at the traffic lights, my car purring like a panther, ready to react instantly to the green light. Not long before, the same car used to cough and die, its puttering engine refusing to idle. The difference? One quarter of a turn on a tiny idling screw, made at the right time by a handy husband with sufficient knowledge of car maintenance.

Shouldn't we now be equally keen to care about the smooth running of the lives of those around us, as a mechanic is to keep cars on the road? Even if we face dirt, expense, fatigue, misunderstanding or discouragement, let us never forget that just as cars are made to run, so people are made to live.

God forbid that we should be less keen, less intent and less persistent than a mechanic!

Letter 2

Dear Mark and Sarah

Thank you for responding so promptly and encouraging me to continue writing. You ask so many questions that I hardly know where to begin to answer them, so I'll start with telling you a little of the background connected with my intercession for children. Then you'll be able to follow the steps which led to the situation as it is now, and gain some insight into the way in which I now minister. As I continue to write, I will highlight some of the most significant discoveries and insights.

My friends and I had not gone very far along the road before we were faced with the problem of the place of 'evil' in the situations which we encountered. That evil is present and operative cannot be denied. Even the brightest rose-coloured spectacles cannot convince the most optimistic and gullible person that everything is the best, in the best of all possible worlds! When one can see destruction, it is natural to look for a destroyer. In fact, it is probably true to say that the inability to recognise the activities of evil and to deal with them effectively, is the most significant factor in the non-improvement of many people who are prayed for.

Everyone has a distaste for being considered a 'demon-hunter' and it is certainly regrettable when problems which plainly need medical, psychiatric or sacramental ministry, are indiscriminately blamed on to the devil, and are handled accordingly. Sometimes the patient has been left floundering even more deeply in the mire of his distress.

So how did Jesus and His disciples deal with 'deliverance' or the 'setting free' of a person from the influence of evil forces, in instances where the person appeared to be in the grip of something against which his own effort, or the efforts of his friends and family seemed to be powerless?

The scriptures plainly refer to evil spirits and record that Jesus spoke to them and ordered them to leave. The disciples did the same thing, using His Name as their authority. Take a hypothetical case. One hears of a child who is jealous of the new addition to the family and who waits for his opportunity to tip the baby out of its crib or to hit it over the head with the nearest hard toy. What are we to think? Observed behaviour has told us that he is reacting to a threat to his own security. He is trying to eliminate the rival for his parent's affection.

In the average household he is punished somehow for behaving in this way. He cannot avoid his parent's displeasure, which they make plain in both word and deed, in order to teach him that such conduct is unacceptable. Necessity usually forces him to conform, outwardly at any rate, but I have met middle-aged people who are still battling with the destructive emotions which were driven underground and buried at the time when a new brother or sister was born.

Is it so 'far out' to say that the child is being troubled by a spirit of jealousy, which has its roots in insecurity? It appears to simplify a great many problems, if, when one knows of a collection of symptoms to which a one-word label may be attached, one can visualise it as an entity. The big breakthrough comes, I believe, when you realise that if you treat it like an entity, it will behave like an entity. That is what Jesus did, and let's face it, His methods seemed to be a great deal more effective than those of our modern-day orthodoxy.

How does this fit in with interceding for children? A very interesting story is recorded in Mark 7:25–30 and also in Matthew 15:21–28 (NEB).

> *Then he left that place and went away into the territory of Tyre. He found a house to stay in, and would have liked to remain unrecognised, but this was impossible. Almost at once a woman whose young daughter was possessed by an unclean spirit heard of him, came in and fell at his feet. (She was a Gentile, a Phoenician of Syria by nationality.) She begged him to drive the spirit out of her daughter. He said to her 'Let the children be satisfied first. It is not fair to take the children's bread and throw it to the dogs.' 'Sir,' she said, 'even the dogs under the table eat the children's scraps.'*
>
> *He said to her, 'For saying that, you may go home content; the unclean spirit has gone out of your daughter.' And when she returned home, she found the child lying in bed; the spirit had left her.*

This story has been read, told and re-told thousands of times, but folk get so side-tracked arguing about the children's bread and the lady's faith that attention is diverted from what Jesus actually did. What did He do? He dismissed an evil spirit from a distance!

So it is not always necessary to have the person present in order to forbid a destructive force to operate in his or her life. If one believes it can be done from a distance, then it can be done from a distance – at least with a child. It would appear, from my experience, that if a person is adult and capable of cooperating and really wants to be free, then a degree of cooperation seems to be necessary. It the person is mentally ill, senile, or a child, they are entitled to our care and protection and we can act for them, even from a distance. The most difficult people to decide about are teenagers, who behave like children one moment and like adults the next. But you can always try. You can lose nothing and the young person may gain a great deal.

To return to the very young, how do we know when it is something evil troubling them and how do we know what it is? How did the Syro-Phoenician lady know that the spirit had left her daughter? The child must have looked different, or behaved differently, or both. We have no way of knowing what the 'unclean' spirit was in the story. All we know is that Jesus spoke the word from where He was, the mother believed it and her own observation later confirmed that it was so.

You will find before too long, that observation of behaviour is the key which will open many doors. Children who cannot talk or whose vocabularies are limited, communicate by action and gesture. My small grand-daughter is a past-master at it. Her uncle gave her a miniature armchair for Christmas. She was eleven months old at the time. When I visited the house she grabbed my finger and pulled. (Come with me.) She jiggled up and down, slapping her thighs. (I am very pleased.) She pointed to the chair and patted the seat. (See what I've got!) Then she wriggled her small behind into the seat, folded her arms and peered unblinkingly in the direction of the television. Who said she couldn't talk? Nothing could be plainer.

Many behavioural signs are not always so straight-forward. Frustration will cause one child to scream and kick in a tantrum, another child to pick up and throw the nearest thing or kick another child, and yet another to refuse to eat, sometimes with tears, sometimes without.

A lad with whom I have recently had dealings, gets up every night after his mother has opened the windows, and goes around shutting them all again. Another boy I know lays out all his pencils and pens in rows, graded for size and colour. These are examples of ritual behaviour and they 'say', 'I am feeling insecure. If I do things over and over again in the same way it comforts me. Don't you understand?'

Unfortunately many parents do not understand. They try to break the child of his 'funny habits' and thus deprive his personality of a survival weapon. When a child is well and happy, such habits fade very quickly.

You will see by now how the combination of the healing of memories or of unremembered but damaging incidents known to have occurred before, during or after birth, combined with deliverance ministry 'in absentia', is a powerful and comprehensive weapon against the destruction of body, mind and spirit which many of the small ones are struggling against.

Next week when I write, I will tell you the story of Danny, and you will see for yourselves how marvellously the power of God can work in a child's life if only we will learn how to let Him use us to channel it where it is needed.

Letter 3

Dear Mark and Sarah

I promised to tell you Danny's story this week. I have chosen his story because in the course of ministering to him, just about everything that I have written to you about had to be done. I never met the child in person. All ministry was done by straight intercession. A friend of mine was the contact, and she and I interceded together.

Danny was an adopted boy and his parents later had a child of their own. His natural mother was both intellectually handicapped and epileptic. She was just thirteen years old when he was born, and his father was an elderly man. You may raise your hands in horror, but these things do go on all the time, and the miracle was that Danny was born relatively normal. During the first few months of his life he went from hospital to a series of foster homes. The last of these homes was bad and the child was neglected and unfed.

Eventually the neighbours called the police and the baby was taken into care, a pathetic little scrap of humanity who weighed a mere fourteen pounds at the age of one year. He was later adopted by the couple who became for him, Mum and Dad. They are fine people who were convinced that if only the child had enough love, then everything would work out right.

They loved him, wisely and well, but everything did not

work out right. Persuading him to eat was a constant battle. Danny spat out his food and Mother spooned more in. Danny reluctantly began to eat, but his behaviour problems increased. He barely grew at all and was described as hyperactive. My friend said he was like a little old man. He had been under all sorts of treatment but apart from the temporary quietening effect of tranquillising medication, nothing seemed to help. He was by this time at school, and in difficulties. His behaviour was ritualistic to the point of eccentricity. He had a curious disregard for any kind of danger and appeared not to mind when he was nearly run over by vehicles.

My friend and I agreed to pray, but where does one begin? I was going over in my mind what we had learned about his life so far, when these words came to me. 'Hyperactivity equals fear of stillness, equals fear of silence, equals fear of death.'

How strange, when he appeared not to be at all frightened of death. I am not saying that this has significance for any other cases of hyperactivity. I am merely saying that this is what I was told about this particular child. We set a date for the intercession and met together. We always begin by affirming the presence of God and remind ourselves that where the light is shining there can be no harmful darkness. We thank Him for this light, the light of His presence. We ask, in Jesus' Name, for the protecting power of the Lord to be upon us and our homes and families. Then being assured by our faith in the promises of scripture that it is indeed so, we begin.

In this case, we remembered the circumstances of his conception and claimed the forgiveness of God on behalf of his natural parents, who had, by their action, begun a human life with no apparent thought for the future well-being of that life. Perhaps one sinned in ignorance and the other in weakness. Who knows? In asking for such forgiveness we have the example of Jesus who prayed for those who were to kill Him, 'Father, forgive them, they know not what they do.' Then we asked that Jesus, the Lord of time, would retrace the steps of the years and would comfort the bewildered young woman through the months of pregnancy and the hours of birth, and we pictured it happening. We asked that the hands which held the child when he was born would indeed be the kind and compassionate hands of Christ. This we 'saw' in our mind's eye. We visualised Jesus Himself standing near to the child and blessing him – compensating for the insecurity brought about by the circumstances of his birth and early life. We covered everything we could think of, reversing mentally, any adverse or inhibiting influence. We stated these things in words and claimed by faith that the opposite state of affairs should begin to come about.

Then it came to me that there was a destructive entity at work – an evil force. When the child, at the age of five months, had lain in his cot neglected and half-starved, the wish to die had entered his life. So he drank his milk and later ate solid food only with great reluctance. He did not really want to live. This obviously explained his feeding problems. Remember that, physically speaking, the mother had won the battle over food. She had, by her love and persistence, nourished him in spite of himself. The refusal to eat was acting out 'I do not want to live,' and the hyperactivity was saying, 'there is an urge towards death in me and it scares me.'

When the force which was attempting to bring about his death through inadequate nourishment was thwarted by the mother, it changed its tactics and tried something new – a carelessness concerning danger – which, sooner or later would have brought about his death through accident. Even the hyperactive behaviour was of great significance, as it became apparent to us that the very means by which his problem was being shown to us was, in itself, wearing him out before his time. What a mess! After our preliminary prayers I 'spoke' to this entity. I was not even sure what to call it. To all intents and purposes I was addressing thin air, but just as we know that God hears us when we speak, so I knew that 'it' could hear me.

I said, 'You spirit of death in Danny, I speak to you in the Name of Jesus Christ, Son of God, and I tell you that your presence has been discovered and that you have no right to be in his life. This child is under the care and protection of Jesus and you are an intruder. I now dismiss you into the hands of Jesus, and I tell you, in His Name, to leave this boy now, and I forbid you to return.'

We moved back from ministry into prayer and asked that there would be, in this lad's life from now on, a great joy in living – an enthusiasm for life – so that he would daily grow to be more optimistic and forward-looking. We prayed that God's Holy Spirit would alert him to situations containing an element of danger and that He would guard and guide the child everywhere he went and in everything he did. We prayed that as he became more settled and secure, the eccentric behaviour which had characterised him would diminish and eventually fall away, and that the boy would grow into the person that God meant him to be. My friend 'agreed' with me and endorsed my prayer. The scriptures say that if we agree together about what we ask, then we can expect it to be done.

There were more details we prayed about, many of which I have now forgotten. I can remember though, that it took us over two hours, and by the time we had finished we were both exhausted from the effort of concentration it taken. All the same, we felt peaceful and happy and waited to see what God would do.

Let me tell you, He did plenty! Danny's behaviour quickly showed a marked improvement. He began to eat and sleep, work and play like any other lad. His school work started to improve and his interaction with his family and with other children rapidly changed for the better. Then there was the day when my friend phoned me and said, 'Guess what – he's growing!' He apparently grew several inches in as many months and no longer gave the impression of being a wizened little old man.

After some time we lost touch until a little while ago when the mother rang my friend concerning another matter. We discovered he has continued to improve and has never looked back. Praise the Lord!

I chose to tell you Danny's story because it is an instance of the very bad changing to the very good. One always chooses an appropriate example to emphasise a point, but there have been many other children whose problems were not as severe. But as you can see from this story, the combination of the healing of the memories plus deliverance 'in absentia' brought about a really spectacular breakthrough.

When one gets involved in this kind of ministry, there are always those say, 'But how do you know that it was the intercession which altered the situation? He might have got better anyway.' True. But he had not done so up to that time, despite many treatments. It is, after all, God who is the power behind all healing isn't it? It was just that His methods this time included the use of our faith and our prayers. It is indisputable that changes did occur. The only answer to the question 'how do you know?' is the answer of the collective weight of many examples. If we were to tell one such story, there is room for doubt, maybe, but if we tell fifty other stories of a similar kind, then the possibility of the changes being brought about by other means, decreases with each story told.

This questioning is quite in order and is to be expected. Scripture says that we should learn to give proper answers to people's questions. We are to treat their doubts with respect. It seems to me there is no particular virtue in being naively credulous. There does seem to be much more virtue in being increasingly curious. 'Why?' and 'How?' are valuable questions so long as we don't refuse to accept valid evidence just because we have not yet answered these questions to our personal satisfaction. I often think of dear old Doubting Thomas, who has been labelled the patron saint of the twentieth-century. The picture that has been drawn of him is of the perpetual sceptic. I have always felt sorry for the poor man. It seems to me that in having doubts and voicing them, he was only being Mr Average

Man. When he did become sure, he became very, very sure – irrevocably and utterly sure. *'My Lord and my God!'* is not exactly the cry of a sceptic, is it? Still, he took a while to get that far. So did we and so do most people.

Perhaps we all need to remember to be as patient with one another's stumbing progress as God is with ours.

Next time I will tell you about Rachel, a beautiful little girl who didn't want to grow up.

Letter 4

Dear Mark and Sarah

I promised this time to tell you about Rachel. I have, in my desk drawer, a bundle of letters. Rachel's father who lives in another city, used to write to me every month to report about her progress. He and his wife were unaware at the time, but each letter provided me with the next clue as to how to continue the intercession.

The story begins when Rachel was eight years old. She was a beautiful looking little girl but her behaviour had her parents just about at their wits' end. She seemed unable to accept other people, including her own family. She was hostile towards everything and everybody and was unbelievably perverse. She repeatedly frightened her parents by saying, 'I don't want to grow up, I want to die, I want to die.' Like Danny, she too was reckless and heedless of danger. Constant vigilance was needed to ensure her safety. Her parents consulted the Education Board psychologist and the family doctor. They did their best but there seemed to be no improvement. I had no idea that things were so bad until we called to see her parents when we visited their city. During the course of conversation it all came out.

After we returned home it came to me that there must be something radically wrong in her past, so I wrote to my friends outlining the broad principles under which I was working, and saying that if they were agreeable, I would intercede. Their own minister and his wife had also agreed to pray.

It is often preferable for someone outside of the immediate family to do the intercession. Parents, who are living every day with the same set of problems, have great difficulty in visualising the situation as ever being any different, and somebody, somewhere, must be able to 'see' things changed. In fact, constantly 'seeing things changed' is faith in action.

In this family, the little girl's arrival – unlike that of poor Danny – had been eagerly anticipated. She had been longed for and loved before she was even born. Her parents were well-balanced, sensible people with a stable outlook on life, a deep faith in God and a great loyalty to their church. What had gone wrong? I pondered, prayed and slept on it. As far as I could see, the way in which the parents had handled her had been exceptionally wise and understanding and there was nothing that they were aware of, which could have caused their small daughter's problems. I knew, from reported information, that certain attitudes and reactions which she displayed had become deeply entrenched in her life. They had become habitual for her and she was unable to react in any other way. How far back had these habits commenced? When had this hostile and antagonistic streak first begun to show itself?

It all went back to the time of her birth. The circumstances were these.

She had been a premature baby, born only after a prolonged and difficult labour. The child was, of necessity, taken from mother and placed in intensive care, where she remained for some time. As I prayed about her birth I felt a wave of anger sweep over me, and it dawned that I was being shown, through my own emotional reaction, what the child had felt at the time.

Wasn't it strange? If she could have spoken she would have said, 'I hate this place, I hate these people. They've taken me from my mother. If this is "the world", I don't like it. I don't want to live here. Why can't I go back to where it was warm and safe? All these people are to blame and so are my mother and father for letting it happen. People are not to be trusted. I hate people!'

So the little one struggled on. When she did go to her mother, how could she know whether or not she would be whisked away again? It had happened before, hadn't it? I did this intercession alone, after taking the phone off the hook.

It is strange how often it will ring when one is trying to pray. I always speak aloud in order to help my concentration not to wander. You will remember the scripture that says 'He shall have whatsoever he saith.' How important to make what we say clear and definite, so that we can set our faith to work on it.

Anyhow, I began to pray, mentally 'seeing' Jesus present with her in her small incubator, so that she was never alone. I asked that His love would cancel out and reverse all the negatives in this young life. Over a period of eleven months her father kept writing. All of her behavioural problems stemmed from that initial rebellion against life and people. 'I want to die' had its roots there, so did suspicion, pessimism and perversity. The 'underlying venom', (her father's phrase) was never far below the surface. She was acting out, in her behaviour, that which had become seared into her 'deep mind' so long ago.

I began the intercession in December, dealing with suicide and anger. The minister and his wife probably began about the same time. February's letter says, 'Please continue, for she is by no means out of bondage.' March's report says says, 'She doesn't say she wants to die any more but her conduct is still marginal. Her school work and her appetite are a bit better but she is lacking in patience to an extreme degree. She has always been one to fight rest and sleep, no matter how badly needed.'

Again I interceded. I 'spoke' to impatience, restlessness and insomnia and told them that they had no place in the child's life and claimed, in the Name of Jesus, that patience and peace would grow in her and that she would begin to have a more normal sleep pattern. The May report noted some improvement, but said she was still a 'puzzle at times.' After the May report I reinforced everything that I had done before and then stepped way out on limb and spoke to rebellion and ordered it out of her life. The June report says, 'Good news, there is a marked improvement in her attitude. There is also an awareness of other people's rights and interests. Many small things show an inward change from a miserable, destructive, back-biting person into one moving towards the sunshine of love. It is sudden and wonderful. Thank you for your prayers and for your love for her.'

August's letter was much the same. I thanked God that He was at work in her life and kept 'seeing' favourable changes coming about. November 21 brought this news. 'Rachel is going from strength to strength – she is a different child!'

This is only one instance among many that I have chosen to tell you about. I have kept records for several years now. It is exciting to see God at work. After many months of dealing with disturbed children along these lines, I came to see that a combination of healing of memories and deliverance in absentia, produced the most rapid and often the most startling results. As I told you earlier, it appeared that, in most cases, if one could get one's finger on the chief trouble-spot and deal with it, then the accompanying difficulties also cleared up.

It reminds one of a fort being held by a strong and efficient commanding officer. When he is picked off by a sniper's bullet, the remaining troops, now leaderless, surrender very quickly. These chief trouble-spots seem to have begun at various times in the children's lives. Sometimes there were shocks and fears at the time of birth or during babyhood. Later in life it was often an illness, a bad fall, an accident, an operation, the death of a pet, a fright concerning fire, water, vehicles, electric power or unjust punishment or disillusionment, caused by the inconsistency or unpredictability of adults.

Although intercession for children occupied a great deal of time, there have also been numerous adults whose present life has been adversely affected by incidents occurring in childhood. In August of last year I was asked to speak at a Health Worker's Retreat which was organized by some Christian Medical Students. I spoke about 'Intercession and Children' but purposely looked up some stories about adults being affected by traumata happening when they were children. Some could remember the events. Others could not. Such things are no problem to the Holy Spirit. I chose to tell them about one of each.

So, next week I'll tell you about Anna and her baby, and perhaps after that, I could tell you about Margaret and her fear of heights. Later we had better have a question and answer session, as I see from your letter that there are many things which interest you.

Letter 5

Dear Mark and Sarah

Today you will read the story of Anna. Anna was referred to me by a friend who knew that I was ministering along the lines I've been telling you about. He did not know what her problem was as she had told nobody but her husband. All he knew was that she needed help. She was a young mother with three children, two girls and a baby boy several months old. After we had chatted for a while she broke down and cried while trying to tell me her problem.

'I'm so ashamed,' she said. 'I hate to have to tell anyone about it but I shall go mad if something isn't done. The truth is – I hate my baby. I just can't stand the sight of him. When I have to feed him I'm nearly sick. I don't understand it. We wanted a boy so much. We were thrilled when he was born. I wasn't like this with the girls. My husband has been so patient but he doesn't understand it either. Now I've told you, you'll think I'm a terrible mother and so I am. I think I must be going mad.'

She felt guilty, ashamed and frightened. She had gone over and over everything and could find no reason for her feelings. I explained to her that if it had been caused by something in the past which she had forgotten, then we could ask the Lord that, if it were right for her, He would show us what it was, so that we could bring it into the light of day and have it put right. She agreed to this and I began to pray, covering her life in 'blocks' of three years at a time. When we came to the age bracket from six to nine years, something began to happen.

In my mind's eye was a picture. There were two little girls in green dresses with white spots, and white socks. One was cowering against a brick wall and the other was lying on the ground crying, in great distress. In the background was the freckled face of a ginger-headed boy, grinning maliciously. I said to her, 'the Lord is showing me something – do you happen to have a twin sister?'

'Yes' she said, 'how do you know?' So I described what I had 'seen'. As I spoke, she remembered the incident. She and her twin sister had been going home from school when the red-haired boy had chased the little girls, captured one of them and with tormenting teasing glee, had dropped a lizard down her back. That was Anna's twin. Anna was furiously angry with the boy – but frightened too. He was tormenting her sister, perhaps she would be next. Panic, fear and anger swept over her and she loathed that boy – she hated him with a deadly hatred.

I explained to her that hatred, no matter what causes it, is destructive, and that if she wanted God to wipe the slate clean, then she should first confess to having harboured it and ask to be forgiven. She agreed to do this. She also agreed to forgive the boy for what he had done to her sister, because she could see that from an adult point of view, he was no worse than any other boy.

I 'declared' that as she had confessed and was herself forgiving, then the forgiveness of God was now hers. We prayed for the twin sister and for any possible damage to her personality which may have come to her through the incident, and for the ginger-headed boy, now grown up of course, wherever he may be. Then God put a thought into my mind. It must have been Him because I wouldn't have thought of it myself in a million years. I said, 'Tell me, what colour hair has your son got?'

She went as white as a sheet and said 'He's a red-head. The girls are both dark but he's a real copper-top.' She had seen the connection. The small girl who had hated a teasing red-haired boy had become the adult woman who hated a small red-haired baby and didn't know why.

The memory was painful and so it had been suppressed, but the emotions associated with it were still very much alive, even though they were buried. All this had been strange and a bit gruelling for her, and while she was resting she went to sleep on my lounge sofa. I crept away and left her. About an hour later she awoke with a glow on her face. 'I'm going home now to my baby,' she said. 'I know I'm cured and I know that I love him.' And so she did. As you can imagine, I was overcome with thankfulness. The love and forgiveness of God had come into a life and made it whole. I had watched it happen. Have you ever stood on holy ground?

Anna's husband wrote to me some weeks later. 'She has told me everything that was said and done,' he wrote, 'and how can I ever thank you? You have given me back my wife. I know it was God who used you and I'm so thankful to Him, but is is a poor show if we can't say thank you to His instruments. I want you to know that I have reached a decision. I've been a casual church attender for many years and did believe in Our Lord, but merely on an intellectual level. Now I've seen Him at work and I know that He's alive and real. We have bought some books on prayer and healing and I have decided that, as a family, we will attend worship every Sunday from now on. What Anna has been through is not the kind of thing that one makes public, but we felt that we needed to tell someone. We asked our priest to call and we told him the whole story. He led us in prayers of thanksgiving. Then he prayed for you and asked God to bless your life and ministry. I thought that you'd like to know. You may tell our story if it will help somebody. Just change the names. Yours sincerely, Bob.'

Let me now continue with Margaret's story. I met this lass at University and we had begun a casual conversation in the chapel reading room. During this conversation she told me about her fear of heights and the difficulties in her life because of it. Being high anywhere brought her up in a cold sweat. Her heart would pound and her hands shake. It was torture for her to climb stairs or steps, and to go up in any kind of elevator gave her the horrors. Things like travelling over a harbour bridge which others take for granted, for her, brought vertigo to the point of nausea. She would steel herself and close her eyes, sitting rigid in bus or car, gripping the seat and enduring the fear. No medical reason for these physical symptoms had been found.

Various well-wishers had advised her to 'get her head examined', to 'snap out of it', to 'pull herself together' or to 'make herself do it' until repetition and familiarity caused her fear to diminish. I wondered how many of those folk would be willing to take their own advice if the positions had been reversed! She felt that nobody understood.

Eventually she stopped talking about it to a large extent, re-arranged her lifestyle, concealed her problem where possible and lived with it where concealment was not possible. She only confided in me on the spur of the moment and I thank God that she did. She was a Christian girl who belonged to an assembly where deliverance ministry was an accepted practice, and with great faith and courage she had gone to her pastor and asked for help. He agreed she shouldn't be like this and said that there could be some spirit troubling her. He ministered to her in the Name of Jesus, and dismissed from her life a 'fear of heights'. They were both sure that she would be released from it and were deeply puzzled when she felt no different and there appeared to be no improvement.

To cut a long story short, I also agreed to pray for her and we set a date. We met in the chapel. I had questioned her about the first time she had ever felt the fear. She remembered the incident vividly. At the age of about six years, she and a companion had climbed up a cliff or rocky hill. The two children had egged each other on, in the way that children do. When they reached the top she turned around and saw where they had come from, and this dreadful fear

came over her that she would never be able to find her way
back again. Here, of course, we have a classic example of a
conditioned response. The fear had first occurred when she
was high up and thereafter, whenever she was high up
again, the same symptoms appeared. You will notice that
it was not the actual height that was so frightening.
Neither was she afraid of falling. It was the prospect of
being unable to find her way back which terrified her.
There was a destructive force in her life, inhibiting her
progress and sapping her joy, and the Lord showed me it
was 'disorientation'. The reason why it had not left her
before, was because it had not been named correctly. I'll
explain.

When one works in absentia and with the children as I
do a great deal of the time, there is no 'patient' present to
question. One therefore has to rely solely on the discernment which God the Holy Spirit gives and I guess I had got
used to doing this. One can look at the symptoms and
presume that one knows. This is purely a mental process. It
may be right, but it is wise to wait for some kind of
confirmation. Even so, with the children, one does not
always get it right first time. We don't always hear God
clearly. If one ministers and there is no improvement, then
one suspects that the discernment has been faulty; because
if one names them correctly and uses the authority of
Jesus' Name, these entities must obey. So you go back and
listen some more. It seems that 'they' know their rights,
but they bank on us not knowing ours!

Anyway, with Margaret, the root cause was not what it
appeared to be. After prayers for God's guidance and
blessing and for our protection, I quietly addressed a 'spirit
of disorientation' and told it that it had no right to be
troubling one whose life had been committed to Jesus.
Then I told it to leave her. Margaret didn't feel anything
but 'light inside'. The result however, was dramatic. She
walked out of the chapel, straight across the campus and
entered the library building. She went into the lift and up
to the third floor. She went to her tutorial class, admiring

the view from up there, a thing she had never been able to do before. That evening she travelled over the harbour bridge, looking down at the water and expressing astonishment at the number of yachts moored at the marina. She was overjoyed. So was I.

Well, I lost touch with her after a while, but some time later a mutual friend reported to me that Margaret was doing well and had never had a return of the 'old trouble'. She had a new boyfriend who was keen on mountaineering and they also enjoyed skiing. All these changes in a girl who had once been afraid of a staircase.

It reminds me of the verse that tells us that if anyone is in Christ, he or she is a new person. You will see from these two stories how these folk, both adult, had great difficulties which stemmed from incidents occurring in childhood.

Margaret had remembered, Anna had not, but God met both of them at the point of their need.

Exciting isn't it?

Letter 6

Dear Mark and Sarah

How nice to hear from you and yes, I will answer some questions for you if I can. You ask what started me off on this pathway and how I have come to be ministering in this way. If you remember, I touched on this earlier in our correspondence when I told you of my days as a Lay Pastor in a busy church. The plight of the children became obvious and it was usually through the conversation of the mothers that I would hear about the needs. As I used to visit around the parish, certain phrases began to be burned into my brain.

Mothers would tell of Barry's bad temper, Joe's jealousy, Tim's tantrums, Elizabeth's exhibitionism, George's greed, Linda's lies, Susan's stealing or Claire's cruelty. They would say something like this, 'He (or she) was no trouble at all until he went to hospital last year. He only had his arm set but after he came home we couldn't do anything with him. He still screams every night but he won't tell us why.' Or, 'She was no trouble at all until the dog was run over. She cried about it for days and then suddenly she wouldn't talk about it any more. I thought, "That's kids for you – they soon forget" – but she began to withdraw into herself, and now nobody can get close to her at all. Her teacher says that at school she has switched off completely and doesn't even hear what is said to her. We're so worried.' Or perhaps one would hear, 'Well, of course, he always was a greedy child. Right from the time he was born. He always wants more. We give him plenty of everything and ample pocket money but still he steals things...'

These, and other variations on the same theme were repeated so often that it depressed me. The common factor in all these instances seemed to be shock. Any shock. One can read some excellent books about 'inner healing' or 'healing of the memories', but almost without exception, they tell of dealing with adults and how to minister to them. As you know, I had had experience with adults myself, years before. Children were different.

No, one does not have to have the child present, or even see him. I discovered this when I experimented with intercessory prayer. Remember the Syro-Phoenician lady's daughter? In many instances, if the child were present, it would simply focus his mind on his problem and this could do more harm than good. God cares for the children, even if they don't know much about Him, and we can do the same. After all, one does not have to explain to a three year old all the processes that have been necessary before his breakfast cereal appears in his plate. One simply calls him to come and eat. He accepts the provision of food without question. Later he may learn a little more about such provision, or he may not. Time alone will tell whether he will ever completely understand it – but in the meantime, we care for him.

Your question regarding the 'commanding officer' in the imaginary fort is most interesting, and yes, we do need to sort this one out. I wrote about the fall of the fort when the officer was killed. You ask 'What can you do if you don't know who the commanding officer is?'

Imagine another fort. This one is commanded by an officer who is not as reckless as the first one. This officer keeps himself screened from view but from time to time his troops are exposed to snipers. Suppose that by patience and tenacity the assailants despatch the troops one at a time. What happens? The officer either surrenders, or is forced out into the open and is killed himself. There is more than one way then, isn't there?

I would say that Rachel's story approximately fits into the second category. The obvious things were dealt with one at a time, and finally the commanding officer also met his match. In the case of Danny, however, the commanding officer was dealt with first, because it was known who he was. The remainder of the troops departed after him.

You say I use the phrase 'It came to me' often, and ask 'How do these things "come" to you?' All I can say is that God's Holy Spirit guides and directs each one of us in the way that suits us best. He seems to guide me a lot through what might be called intuition. I had to learn how to consciously ask to be guided, and then having done that, to believe that it was happening. Then one must be courageous and act on one's 'hunches'.

When dealing with children, one must deduce from clues in the behaviour what the disturbance is, and how it came about. I find that I feed in to my mind all the relevant detail that people report to me. Then I pray that God will sort it out and will bring to my consciousness those things that are important. Sometimes this can happen during sleep, and that which is uppermost in the mind upon wakening, is what needs to be pursued further. Sometimes the scriptures will give one the clue or will confirm what had come into the mind earlier. I rarely get the 'voice in the ear' type of guidance which I know comes to some folk. Rather it is a recurring impression which persists. Sometimes I 'see' things. You will remember from the old days that ever since my experience of the fullness of the Holy Spirit, the visionary faculty has been with me. Perhaps in the future, a little more explanation while I am writing to you would be helpful.

You ask how I 'know' things. God tells me, one way or another. There are times when we never know. Maybe we do not hear Him properly, or perhaps we have asked to be shown something and it is not the right time for it to be known. I have given this quite a bit of thought, as it seems to be important to you, and I make this comment. In our human weakness and stupidity, we tend to jump to conclusions and to take what we see on the surface as being the important things. Our minds seem to revert to past experiences and of course this is not always wrong. It is only wrong if we become inflexible in our thinking and so close our ears to the voice of the Lord.

For instance, a couple of years ago I had dealings with one who was troubled by an urge to strip off all her clothes in public. Yes, there was a spiritual force involved, and its name was 'exposure'. This is what any observer saw. But we must go one step further and ask, 'Why is it there?' In this instance, fear was the control spirit. The lady imagined, without any real grounds, that her husband was looking elsewhere and she was afraid. In her doubt and desperation she was acting out – 'Look at me! See, I'm still shapely aren't I?' Shortly afterwards a friend of mine was involved with a lady who was similarly afflicted. How easy it would have been to say to oneself, 'It was exposure and fear last time, the symptoms are the same, it surely must be the same this time.' But it was not.

Just as each person is valuable and loved by God, so each one is entitled to our unbiased attention. We are not to go flashing hasty discernments around, and in the process, perhaps wounding a fellow human being. Only God knows whether or not it is the same. How much better to listen to Him afresh each time. In this instance my mind played with the question, 'Why do people strip off their clothes?' Within three days I had seen a small child at the beach climb out of his pants because they restricted him, a young girl swimming topless, and a report of a streaker running naked across the grounds at a local cricket match.

People peel off their clothes for all these reasons and many more besides. Our thinking must be open-ended and only when it is can the Holy Spirit speak. If we've already jumped to a conclusion we will never hear Him. There was no exposure and no fear in the case of the second lady. No evil force at all. She was merely acting out, in her rather confused and sad mental state, a deep desire to return to the state of childhood innocence. She wanted to shed the 'cover-up', the sham and the pretence and the hypocrisy into which the circumstances of her life had led her, and simply to be her real self. A desire for innocence told me that her present state of mind was one of guilt. She needed to know and to be assured of the forgiveness of God, and she was. In less than a month she was over her trouble.

You asked me what was the worst case of a disturbed child I ever had to deal with. Time has now run out so I will wait until next week to tell you about Paul.

Letter 7

Dear Mark and Sarah

For many months after God cured Paul, I could tell nobody about it. There was a kind of awesome feeling inside, because of the knowledge of the terrible suffering that his parents had undergone. It was as though we were each holding our breath and if we tried to tell, then we wouldn't be able to control tears of thankfulness. After a year or more I told a group about him, although I didn't use his real name. If it were your child, you wouldn't want me to either. Last year I told the medical students about him. There was a reason for this. I felt that these young people were being taught a great deal about how to treat symptoms, as of course they must be, but sometimes there seems to be a tendency among them to imagine that when the 'body' is functioning well again, then the patient is cured. Most of our doctors who have been in practice for a long time are very aware that this is not necessarily so. I also told them about Paul because, by all appearances, he was the picture of health. He had lovely eyes and a flawless skin, sturdy limbs and a mop of curls. He was a beautiful boy.

When he was about two and a half his parents noticed that he had a tendency to kill things – bugs, beetles – insects of all kinds. As he grew, he killed anything he could knock down or catch and he became precociously skilful and adept at annihilating lizards and similar-sized creatures. He even appeared with the odd bird. How he caught them nobody knew. His parents tried (in order); ignoring his behaviour hoping it would pass, diversionary tactics to distract him, reasoning and talking with him, and lastly, punishing him. Nothing worked. Unlike most children, who lose interest in a 'corpse' when life and, movement have gone, he seemed to gloat over the bodies. The family goldfish vanished from the bowl and were found, carefully wrapped in silver paper, concealed under his bed. He had received both medical and psychiatric help, but his condition continued to deteriorate. His mother was on edge all day and every day and watched him closely, but he became increasingly evasive. His father was on the verge of an ulcer. Both parents had the horrors thinking about the future. What would become of him?

They tried to conceal his activities from his grandparents and those who loved him, but that was not always possible. So two more families suffered and worried. He killed the guinea pigs belonging to the neighbour's children. He loved to hold creatures under water until they drowned. He deeply resented it when the bodies were taken away from him and he resisted with a strength that was frightening. If he were punished he would cry at first, but then would laugh hysterically. As a last resort his parents bought him a kitten, hoping he would learn to care for it and so come to enjoy living things. While his mother was occupied with a visitor at the door, he vanished. She found him later crouched under the hedge, stroking the dead kitten's fur and crooning to it. He was glassy-eyed and in a semi-trance of ecstacy. He had strangled it.

The parents were becoming frantic. I knew nothing of this until later. The sister-in-law was the only one of the family that I knew, although I had seen the child and his mother, in passing. The climax came when the mother discovered him at the next door house, standing on an upturned bucket. In his hand was the largest stone that he could grasp and this hand was poised over the head of the neighbour's baby, who was asleep outside in his pram. With admirable control, the mother whisked him, screaming and yelling inside, locked the doors and waited until her husband came home.

That was when her control snapped and she poured out all the horror of the past, present and contemplated future, and her grief and despair at raising what she called a 'monster'. Their son was by this time approaching five years of age. She then collapsed into a sobbing, incoherent heap.

The doctor arrived to sedate her. Next came the sister-in-law to hold the fort until the morning when some vital decisions would have to be made. Nobody could take any more. It was the sister-in-law who telephoned me and related most of what I have told you. I promised that I would intercede and left the telephone with very mixed emotions. The stories about his behaviour would leave any mother gasping and nauseated. They were so dreadful and unbelievable and yet they were true. I found that anger swept over me as I knew that the boy was in the grip of something evil and that it was wrecking the lives of his entire family. Then I remembered the Old Testament story of Daniel, when he was asked to interpret the king's dream, *'Be it known unto you, O king, that there is a God in heaven who revealeth secrets – even our God.'*

So I asked the Lord to tell me the name of this spirit in order that I might dismiss it in His Name, and that the boy might be set free. Then I slept. I awakened at just before 3 o'clock in the morning with a strange, strong urge to look in the dictionary. Still half-asleep, I tip-toed past my sleeping husband to the book-case. I flicked the pages while mentally saying 'What do you want to show me Lord?' when my eye and my finger simultaneously landed on a spot. Prefix – 'necro' – corpse, from Greek, *nekros*. On went my eye – necrobiosis, necrogenic, necrology, necromancy, necrophilia, necropolis – I backtracked – necrophilia, the love of corpses!

I knew the word. In my vocabulary it concerned the

performance of erotic acts upon the dead. I'd never heard of such a thing in a child. Never. Still, I had been shown, and that was that. I went through the ministry and dismissal at three in the morning, in whispers, alone in the lounge, addressing 'necrophilia in Paul's life' and telling it in the Name of Jesus to leave the child. I always dismiss spirits into the hands of Jesus, as He is the only one with power over everything in heaven and earth. Who are we to go telling them where to go forever? We only have authority to dismiss them from manifesting here on earth to the detriment of our fellows. What happens in time and eternity is not our business.

I ordered it never to return to him and forbade it to trouble anyone else in his family. Then I prayed that the love of our Creator for all living things would grow in him. Then I slept again. I later learned from the sister-in-law what transpired. The father, after a deeply disturbed night was alerted, before 7 o'clock, by noises which sounded like Paul was rummaging around the house. In deep weariness and utter sadness he left his still sleeping wife and went to investigate. The child was gathering up all his corpses from their hiding places and tipping them into a box. He looked at his father and said, 'Get matches, come.'

Father and son made tracks to the garden incinerator and in silence they crumpled up paper, tipped in the contents of Paul's box, and Father lit the fire. A small hand felt for his. 'Paul better now, Daddy,' piped the child, 'Paul not collect dead things any more never.' Daddy cried. So did I when I heard. The mother slowly recovered, watching the change in her son with almost disbelieving joy.

The boy became a delightful youngster, who has never, from that day to this, knowingly killed anything. Over three years have passed and he has all but forgotten those former days and it is better so. The parents have since had another child which, for them, was an act of faith. I have never known how this entity gained access to the child's mind and life. All I know is that Jesus is Lord. The entity was dismissed and has never returned and the child is now free to grow into the kind of person that he was meant to be.

People have asked me, 'Why don't you just ask God to deal with it?' Well, we do, but Jesus Himself gave His disciples power and authority to do this kind of liberating work and if we are disciples, then the command to preach the gospel and heal the sick applies to us too. A disciple, as you know, is one who is 'under discipline', a learner. I'm sure that we are all expected to learn how to cooperate with God, who will teach us to use the power and authority that He has given. After all, the Bible says that mankind was put on the earth to have dominion over it – to learn how to manage it, in other words.

Paul, even though he was physically healthy, had been a desperately sick child. It is as though the Lord is saying to us, 'My world has become a damaged world, and my people are wounded people. I've been teaching you how so that you can begin to fix it for Me.' Jesus Himself cured people because He loved them. Sometimes He wasn't even thanked. According to His story about the ten lepers, the chances were about one in ten! I wonder whether or not you think that today's statistics are any different.

With Paul, it was straight deliverance in absentia, with healing prayers to follow. After all, it is reasonable to infer that if a spirit had gained access, then there must have been some shock, upheaval or hereditary loop-hole which allowed it in. We don't know what, but God does and we can always ask Him to mend any damaged place. In this instance there was only one spirit present and it was powerful. When it left him his whole life was changed. Amazing, isn't it?

Letter 8

Dear Mark and Sarah

So much has happened since I last wrote to you. Two days ago a Christian lady I will call Vera, called to see me. A friend had sent her. She was extremely upset. She said that she knew her trouble was 'all in my mind, but I think I am under a curse. All the women in our family die when they are thirty-two. I'm thirty-one now – my birthday is next month – and I'm rigid with fear. What's going to happen to me? I haven't got a terminal illness, so I must be going to die in an accident. I'm scared to go out and I'm scared to stay home – scared to do things and scared not to do them. My friend says that you often intercede for people in trouble. Can you do anything to help me?'

So I said, 'Yes, I can.' You will find it is nearly always better to say 'I can' than 'God can', as that can sound like a religious phrase, and most folk have heard them all before and are now suspicious of such words. It is useless at this stage, to try to explain that one can do nothing without God. Later, when they have been helped they express enormous curiosity about the means used. That is the ideal time to do some explaining, not when the person is in dire straits.

So I said 'I'll help you, but you must tell me a little more first.'

It transpired that her mother, grandmother, her only

aunt and her older sister, had all died at the age of thirty-two. The family had commented on the deaths of granny and auntie when the mother had died, so that even as a child she had registered the possibility, even the inevitability, of early death.

It was only after the older sister's death though, that it really began to bother her. The sister was three years older than she was and had died of cancer a couple of years before. As her birthday approached she would awaken in the night in great fear, remembering her sister. Although she was a Christian, her outlook was a little conservative and the concept of evil spirits, to her, meant something straight out of a medieval melodrama, complete with horns and a tail. So I tackled it a different way. I said, 'Have you normally been a fearful person?' She had not. 'Then this fear that you have is not part of the real "you" is it?' It was not. 'Then it is intruding into your mind and life and it is bad for you. Right. We shall write down "fear". Now can you think of any other thing that you can put a name to that shouldn't be there?'

'Well, I guess the whole thing is pretty fatalistic really, but I can't help it,' she said. So we wrote 'fatalism' on the pad. 'Do you know,' I said, 'that the Bible says that the days of our years of three score years and ten but you tell me that yours are going to be one score and twelve. Now I know that some folk do die early from accident or illness but don't you think that we ought to expect the Bible quota?'

'I suppose we should,' she said, 'it's only that in my family it has been different, so I automatically thought that I would be the same as mother and granny and auntie and my sister. Can I change what I think?' 'Well,' I replied, 'we all change what we think, as time and experience show us more, so why shouldn't you? If the Bible says to expect one thing and you have been pressured into thinking something different, then you have been hoodwinked, haven't you?' She conceded the point. 'Deception' was written on the pad. 'Could you manage all right, do you

45

think, if you didn't have this fear, fatalism and deception?'
She was sure she could.

'Now,' I said, 'I want you to think of these things as three
dark shapes floating around your head. Now speak to them
and tell them you don't want them in your life.' 'It seems a
bit silly,' she said, 'but if you think it will do any good, I'll
try.' She did.

'Now,' I said, 'I'm going to tell them to leave you, using
the Name of Jesus as my authority – and they will. Then I
will ask for the light of the presence of God to fill your life
and mind. You just sit there and imagine the light flooding
in. Imagine a dark room with the blinds down and then
you put up the blinds. Where do the shadows go when the
light pours in? Where are the dark shapes then? They have
to go, because you can't have light and darkness at the
same time.'

We went ahead and did just that, and they left her. I
thought for a moment she was going to faint, as the
sudden relaxation after so many months of tension left
her very conscious of her own weakness. Then she said,
'The light is very beautiful – yellow and pale pink. It's
lovely.' God had made His presence known to her in a way
that could not be disputed and which she would always be
able to recall. I smiled. It was lovely.

When she had come down to earth a bit more, I
explained that the only way the shadows could get in
again was if she let them in, and I wrote out a prayer for
her – a prayer of thanksgiving. I've repeated all the
conversation for you so that you can see that there are
many different ways of dealing with the problem of evil.
Just because a person has preconceived ideas and a stereo-
typed model of evil, it need not stop the power of God
from working. Nor need it prevent us, His servants, from
using it. We merely use as much conversational skill as we
can muster and, under the inspiration of the Holy Spirit,
we create an image that they can accept. If I had spoken to
this lady about evil spirits, she couldn't have taken it, but
putting a name to dark shapes and telling them to go away,

was acceptable. She could see it happening in her mind's eye, and this is surely the essence of faith.

It is now a couple of weeks since all this happened. She has taken on a new lease of life and is still walking on cloud nine in the pink and yellow light.

I must tell you also about the lad I mentioned earlier who gets up at night and shuts all the windows. His mother spoke to me on the phone and said that he insists on his room being sprayed with insect killer because the mosquitoes annoy him. Earlier he had said that the noise of the crickets chirping kept him awake. As I continued to pray for the boy, I had a picture in my mind's eye of a very young baby in a crib and flies were buzzing around his head and were settling on his face. I knew then, that at some time during his early life, perhaps before his present parents adopted him, there had been such an occasion. I have prayed about the anger and annoyance the child must have felt, and obviously still feels, where insects are concerned and have pictured Jesus standing there, brushing the flies away. I just know that soon I am going to hear good news about him – that he can sleep in peace and be free from the compulsive ritual which has bothered him for so long.

A few days ago a friend rang. She spoke of another adopted child – a girl aged eight and a half, and of her parents. She and her mother had been at loggerheads from the very beginning. The couple have two older children of their own. Apparently they decided against having more children because of the shocking pregnancies and difficult confinements experienced by the wife. In spite of all that she breastfed her babies for months and she and her husband really do love children. She has been in complete turmoil over her inability to strike any compatible chord with her much-loved and wanted adopted daughter. A real puzzle. Where to begin?

I asked my caller about the early days of the child's adoption and of the attitude of the father towards the little one.

'Oh' she said, 'I don't think you'll find anything wrong there. The father loved her very much. In fact, he thoroughly enjoyed having a baby in the house who was not breastfed. This one was bottle-fed and he fed her as often as he could. He had great fun. He enjoyed being a father even more than when his own two were small.'

Bells began to ring. Contrary to expectations, this is exactly where the root of the problem lay. If we, like any mother had gone through many nauseated months and hour after hour of difficult labour to bring two children into the world, and had followed this with months of the time and care necessary for breast feeding, how would we feel when our husbands got more pleasure and fun from a child who wasn't even ours?

Yes, she had resented it. But sensible, loving, motherly people do not resent a tiny helpless bundle, so she buried her resentment as being an unworthy thought, before it had even registered on her consciousness properly. It had cost her a great deal to bear her own children. They were her 'gift' to her husband. Her gift was valued less than she expected and a strange imported gift was valued more, and she was wounded.

'But,' she reasoned with herself, 'decent people love and care for babies, no matter what. Decent people don't admit to such feelings, or begrudge their husbands the pleasure and fun which was limited at previous times. Decent people ought to be ashamed of harbouring resentment.' And so she was. Although she was almost unaware of it being there, it had come out in small, unobtrusive ways. The child had sensed it and reacted against it. There you have the problem.

My friend and her husband came to see me and we had an intercession session. I began, covering everything that I knew had happened, or that I suspected may have happened up to the age of five years. Shelley continued as far as eight and a half years and then Rick offered prayers about the whole family and their action and interaction with each other. Already we had a report telling of improvement.

Next, I had a phone call about another girl of four and a half. She was the eldest of a family of three, the first two being adopted. The information given to me was a bit sketchy but the child's sleepless nights and bad dreams were wearing the whole family down. When I began to pray, saying 'Lord, what am I supposed to do?' quite involuntarily I began to weep and double up with pain. You may have heard of someone else who has spoken about this kind of thing. The best way I can describe it is like this.

It is as though one's 'feeling self' is affected by a certain emotion. One's 'knowing self' however, seems to observe it going on, without any impression of reality or permanence. The mind will register pain or fear, anger or jealousy, confusion or loneliness, but the effects of these things just do not bring about any painful aftermath whatsoever on the mind or spirit. I have no quarrel with anyone else who explains it differently. This is just what happens to me. It seems to be a way which God has of telling us, by sense impression, what the root cause is of the problem with which we have to deal.

So I rang Chris and said, 'Look, about that little girl. I keep getting this "pain" thing. Somewhere along the line this child has been deeply wounded, both spiritually and emotionally – perhaps physically too.' Chris had learned more about the family in the meantime. The child had been a troublesome, sleepless baby, and the father, having been rigidly raised himself, used to become angry when she wouldn't sleep. He tended to be rough with her, throwing her into the bed in his frustration and not realising that his own conduct was compounding the problem.

He has since had a change of heart – but what about the damage? The little one was able to tell her parents about one of the terrifying dreams. Before her was a beehive. She knew that one got honey from bees and that honey was nice. She opened up the hive to get the honey and found a little girl in there who couldn't get out. She was being stung by the bees. That little girl was herself. She just had to sit there and 'endure' and she felt that she could stand no more. Then she would wake up. Now, have you ever had anything to do with dream symbols? If you can crack the code then you have the key to the cause of certain behaviour. This is particularly significant in the case of small children who lack an adequate vocabulary. It is communication by images. In this instance, the little girl had expected life to be good. She had expected love, care and understanding. This was 'honey'. Life however, did not turn out to be good. There was misunderstanding, there was little patience, there was rough handling, physical pain and love on a 'bargain basis', i.e. 'You perform the way I want you to and I'll love you. If you don't, I'll be angry and reject you.'

These were the 'stings' from which there appeared to be no escape. By interpreting the dream symbols I was able to tell Chris that the child was suffering from insecurity, because of the conditional nature of the love offered and the unpredictability of her father's conduct. She was also afraid of him and afraid of life itself but she was powerless to do anything but endure more of the same – and she feared that too. She had also been deceived because she had accepted that nothing could be changed. The over-riding emotion was that of disappointment. The tears which I shed in 'vicarious diagnosis' were tears of disappointment.

I have been asked what the difference is between grief and disappointment. We could say that grief is deep sorrow and by common usage, is associated with loss. Disappointment is deep sorrow caused by unfulfilled expectation. Broadly speaking, in one case we are sad because of what we once had and have now lost, and in the other case we are sad because of what we know about, thought we were going to get, but never had.

It is helpful when trying to discern a situation accurately, to understand the distinction between different words. A good example is the words 'deception' and 'delusion'. They are often seen as meaning the same thing, but they are not, although they usually go hand in hand. Perhaps it would be helpful to say that in one case we are hoodwinked by our senses and in the other by our reason. Imagine a children's party. The magician pulls a rabbit out of a hat – at least, that is what our senses tell us. If we believed it, we would be both deluded and deceived. The 'reason' though, may reject what the 'senses' say. We may argue to ourselves that rabbits don't come out of hats and that the magician has tricked us into 'seeing' that they do. This is why I call them twins, because although one can be hoodwinked into believing an erroneous set of circumstances to be true, those circumstances have probably arisen in the mind through what the senses of hearing and sight, or both, have registered.

Next time I'll write about the problem of anorexia nervosa.

Letter 9

Dear Mark and Sarah

I had better start this week by telling you what anorexia nervosa is. The word anorexic means 'without appetite' and nervosa tells us that the disturbance is 'nervous' or psychological in origin. It seems to chiefly disturb teenage girls, although boys now seem to be increasingly affected, as have been older age groups. I will try to condense for you what it took me several years to learn.

Those with this affliction have an inability to nourish themselves. They have no appetite most of the time – apart from the occasional eating binge – and when they eat, they feel guilty. This means they must rush away to exercise in order to use up energy. Self-induced vomiting and strong laxatives are often resorted to, in order to get the food out of their system. The anorexic seems to believe that if slim is beautiful then skinny is more beautiful. She may be hideously gaunt but she is deluded about her own body size and shape. Others have had their eating function disturbed, either by some traumatic event or by some long-standing set of circumstances. At least, this is how it has appeared to me. The girls are often highly intelligent – sometimes coming from families where a frightening degree of competence is expected from them. They frequently have a streak of perfectionism in their characters and some of them have an almost morbid fear of maturity.

They can be forcibly fed of course, but unless the underlying cause is discovered and dealt with, regression is bound to occur.

Families react differently too. Some families are heartbroken at seeing a beautiful and talented child shrink to skin and bone. Others react with anger, doubting the patient's sanity and berating the doctors and psychiatrists for 'doing nothing'.

Anyway, let's look at such cases. Here we have rampant destruction of life at its most blatant. As I told you before, where there is destruction, look for a destroyer. When I first encountered the malady I was very ignorant about it, but ignorant or not, I recognised a destroyer at work. A lady whom I knew came forward for prayer at one of the local healing services. Her niece, at the time, was in hospital with anorexia nervosa and she was alarmed to notice the same symptoms appearing in her own daughter, who was sixteen at the time. Jenny was a tall girl, who, being unable to eat, was fading away to a shadow.

It transpired that the onset of her symptoms was precipitated by a conversation which had occurred much earlier, at school. Jenny's girlfriend's mother had been to a fortune-teller who had said that one of this lady's daughter's friends would be involved in a terrible accident and would be crippled for life. The silly woman told her daughter, who in turn told Jenny, who immediately imagined that the dire prediction applied to herself. Her inner self 'said' to her body, 'Better to die now than to live on as a cripple.' She could not eat. Fear had been planted in her mind and had begun to destroy her. Fear usually destroys appetite, although with most of us it is only a temporary state.

I spent a sleepless night discerning the spirits involved. Late the next morning – a Saturday – I went to see a friend and his wife and told them the story and the facts as they had been related to me. He thought for a while and then listed the same things I had written down! We were in agreement. As well as having a 'fear of the future' Jenny

53

was deceived. She had believed as inevitable, that which was purely speculative. She was deluded, as it was through her hearing that the hood-winking was done. The spirit responsible for this had operated through the fortune-teller and its name was 'false prophecy'.

We ministered in absentia and ordered these spirits to leave in Jesus' Name, and then we prayed for the opposite qualities to live and grow in her. Instead of the fear of the future, optimism – instead of deception and delusion, true clarity of mind and senses – instead of false prophecy, confidence in the prospect of a good life. I found very early on in this ministry, that it good to 'sweep the house' but unless you 'see' those rooms filled with something good, the patient is seriously disadvantaged and progress is often slow. It is necessary I think, to follow a minus with a plus.

I went home and slept. One often gets sleepy after this kind of ministry. I saw the mother at church on Sunday. Jenny had begun to eat in the late afternoon of the previous day, about three hours after our ministry session. She began with milk and ice-cream. In a day or two she was eating normally and put on fourteen pounds in two weeks. This was all so awesome – but my confidence is growing. God will do what He said He will do, but we have to get ourselves into gear to believe it, and then we have to learn to see it happening in our mind's eye.

Having seen this lass come right, the aunt and I were encouraged to intercede for the niece who, incidentally, I never met in person. Auntie and I exchanged information by telephone. Here was a different set of circumstances entirely. This girl was intellectually brilliant, as was her sister also. The parents set high standards and it was in this atmosphere that the girls had grown up. These exceptionlly clever girls had a dreadful fear of failure. It was a real problem for them. Having once achieved well and climbed to the top of the academic tree, where else is there to go but down? If one is used to A+ passes, then a mere A constitutes a falling standard, and so they are driven relentlessly on. The girl came out of hospital and made slow recovery. I never did get my finger on the key factor in her case, but I believed she would get better and she did. Three years later her picture appeared in one of the local papers. She looked beautiful and bonny and was the winner of yet another scholarship.

At the time when this lass was hospitalised, she made friends with another anorexic and the her details were related to me. I never met this girl either, but she too, was cured. Anorexia nervosa cases are instances where I find it easier to believe for wholeness and health when I have not seen the gaunt and ill patient. Some days before I heard about the lass, I was reading Psalm 107, parts of verses 17–20 (New English Bible).

> *'Some were fools – they took to rebellious ways – they sickened at the sight of food and drew near to the very gates of death – He sent His word to heal them and bring them alive out of the pit of death – Let them thank the Lord for His enduring love.'*

I telephoned my friend Nita, who sometimes ministers with me. I said, 'Do you know, I have just found a perfect description of an anorexic case and rebellion was at the bottom of it. I just know that the next one we hear about will have rebellion at the bottom of it.' And so it proved to be. Rosalie was indeed 'near to the gates of death'. At seventeen, she weighed a mere sixty-three pounds! This was her story.

Her mother had died the year before and her father had buried himself in his business affairs in order to cope with his own grief. There were no brothers or sisters and the stage was set for a lonely girl to become very angry with life. Her 'inner self' said to her 'Life has dealt you a dirty deal – why stay? It's nothing but a drag from beginning to end. People you love die and leave you, and nobody cares.' The key was rebellion, but we also had a 'fear of the future' and an enormous dollop of 'self-pity'.

We ministered in our usual style, but we dealt with

observable manifestations first and then went back into the past with general prayer covering her early life, in case there was anything there which needed attention and which, if left unattended, would prevent the maximum improvement taking place. Then we went home and believed that what we were believing for was, even at that moment, in the process of coming about. We thanked God that He could be trusted to care for this needy lass.

She began to improve – the same day, I discovered later. We had prayed through the time of her mother's death, asking the Lord to comfort the sorrow and transform the grief. We had also claimed her deliverance from the spirits which I listed for you. We spoke to them and told them to leave. Before long, we heard that she had come out of hospital (weighing ninety-four pounds), and had left to attend University. There has, to the best of my knowledge, been no regression.

The case of Carol was very different. A friend of mine, an elderly minister, telephoned me about Carol. Her parents attended his church. The information was this. The lass was inclined to be plump and had gone on a diet, finding after a while that the obsession had taken over her mind and she could hardly eat at all. The mother was a rather domineering person who, in her sincere efforts to do the best for her children, had always been too conscientious about the 'management' of the family members. The boys had broken free but the daughter could not. She felt that the only thing in her life that had been left for her to control, was the amount that she ate. So we have different things at work here, from different motivations.

Firstly, she was deceived. She believed that nobody could love her the way she was – a little plump – and that in order to gain love, she must change her shape and become beautiful and slim. There was fear (of not being loved) and vanity was also present. I did the intercession alone on December 6th, and by Christmas day she was well enough to be allowed home for a few days. She returned to the hospital and made slow progress. It was five months before she was really well. After the quick recovery of the others it could have been disappointing that this girl took so long to recover, but over the years I have become firmly convinced that when we commit such things into the hands of God, then we must believe that that is where they are, and that there are good reasons for the apparent slowness. In this instance Carol's medical advisors no doubt picked up, as I did, the rather unhealthy relationship between mother and daughter. A 'managing', or controlling mother, is the last thing a teenager needs when she is struggling to learn how to control her own life. In Carol's case, a long separation from her family and from her mother in particular, gave her a chance to be herself.

For a girl who has everything controlled for her, freedom is a highly desirable, but extremely frightening thing, and it takes time to believe in it, adjust to it, and be confident about it. I also included the mother in my intercession – that God would open her eyes concerning the effects of her own behaviour. She, of course, would have done anything and everything for the wellbeing of her family. The family didn't need such thorough care, but she evidently needed to give it. This pointed to something in her own life – perhaps a driving need to prove her own usefulness by having others dependent on her, or perhaps an urge to feel power by manipulating others. Who knows? Anyway, Carol recovered and was freed from this vicious and destructive malady.

Letter 10

Dear Mark and Sarah

I must tell you – it's so exciting! Do you remember that I told you about seeing a vision of a baby with flies buzzing around its face? It happened while I was interceding for an adopted boy who was in difficulties. Well, I met the mother at the shops the other day and she says that he is so much better that they can hardly believe it. The family went away at Easter time in their caravan and he slept outside under the awning, where, of all places, he would be more likely to encounter insects than anywhere else. It appears that his one-time frustration and annoyance with insects, and the ensuing insomnia, have no effect on him at all now, and consequently he is much easier to live with and has begun to progress well at school too. The other day one of my friends called to see me and I enquired about the little girl who dreamt about the beehive and about being unable to get away from the stings. These days she sleeps right through the night and has no nightmares at all. I'm just so happy and grateful to God.

You mention that distance 'seems to be no object' as far as intercession is concerned and this is true. For many years I have contributed to the support of an Indian girl, and have gained a great deal of pleasure from her letters, which she used to write mainly in Tamil. Now her English is quite good and neither of us need translators. Susheela – Susie for short – was brought up in a girls home in Madras. Until her teenage years I had always had glowing reports about her schoolwork and progress in general. Then came a letter saying Susie was 'so difficult and moody, bullying and rough, such a trial to the staff and the other girls.'

I read part of the letter to the prayer group which I was attending at the time and they joined me in prayers for Susie. A few days later it came to me that I should minister healing of memories for her, which I did. That was on 13 May. One often finds that it is when a young person comes to teenage years that all kinds of things start to bother them. Sometimes they are connected with events which have been buried deep, even from babyhood. All I knew about her childhood was that her father was dead and that her mother had abandoned her when she was four years old because she could no longer care for her child. Susie was found at the door of a police station and was eventually placed in care at the Home.

I began to pray through from conception to three years – including any shocks which may have occurred during the mother's pregnancy and Susie's birth. Fears became apparent. The usual ones for babies – falling, loud noises, pain etc. I continued in blocks of three years. Anyone who is abandoned would be afraid and lonely. They would feel rejected and isolated. Why should Susie be any different? Later on, when she became aware that other people had homes and parents and families and she had not, misery, resentment and envy would set in. This can lead to depression, discontent and anger. I sensed, in my spirit, the bewilderment of the little four-year-old, precipitated suddenly among strangers, fearful and alone, wanting her mother. The tears flowed and I let them.

Meanwhile, the other half of me was registering the emotions that I have listed for you. I knew that these were things which were troubling Susie and I prayed and ministered accordingly, speaking to fear, envy, anger and resentment, telling them to leave. Then I 'cancelled' out the minor things by reversing them and asking in faith for the opposite qualities to live and grow in her. Then I wrote to the Principal of the Home and told her what I had done. I had no idea how she would receive it, but I wanted God to get the credit when Susie changed and improved. The Bible says that certain signs follow those that believe. I believed that she would change for the better. So I said so. Had I waited until a change was reported and then written, would it have carried the same weight? I doubt it. It is no good expecting the signs to precede you.

In August I received a letter from the Principal. It began 'Such a change has come over Susheela; I think from about early June. I feel sure that the power of your prayers surely started the change in her...' etc. etc. As the intercession was done about the middle of May, it was probably a couple of weeks before the staff and the other girls noticed anything that they could call a stable improvement. She's been fine ever since. Praise the Lord.

Later on an Indian friend told me of another lass – anorexia nervosa is no respecter of persons or nationalities. I also prayed for this girl who had grown thinner by the day and could eat virtually nothing. From what I was told, she had had a rather protected childhood and it came to me that her lack of appetite was due to a psychological disturbance, brought about by shock. She had been injured in an accident and I guess that any sensitive teenager who spent several hours in the casualty department of an Indian hospital would have her eyes well and truly opened. All the flotsam and jetsam of sick and injured humanity would stream by, filling the present with horror and the future with dread. What a moment for a subtle voice to whisper, 'See what happens when you grow up? See the sickness and the pain? See how dreadful life is? See what you'll be like in ten or twenty years? See! See! See! You don't want to grow up, do you? Of course you don't...' No wonder she couldn't eat.

In prayer, I 're-lived' the time of the accident and the anxious, fearful hours which she lived through while awaiting treatment. I imagined Jesus there with her, comforting and caring. Then I claimed by faith, that it be so. I later heard that she recovered.

Several other anorexia cases came my way. There was Rita, in her early twenties. Her mother had died of cancer. The shock of Rita's teenage pregnancy had coincided with the onset of her mother's illness. Rita married and had her child, but anorexia was rearing its head. Her conscious mind knew that shock does not cause cancer, but the arch-deceiver spoke to her inner self and said, 'You really are rotten, aren't you? You caused your mother's death. She got sick because of what you did. You are not fit to live.' She was both deceived and deluded, but the key was guilt. Very often the patients are unaware of the subleties of their own spiritual bombardment. If they were, perhaps they could reason their way through. In the majority of cases reason does not stand a chance. The feelings are too strong. It is strange how often we take notice of our feelings when our common sense if telling us something quite different. God's Holy Spirit will often reveal to the intercessor the reasons for the feelings. Often it is wise to keep silent about such things. The patient usually has enough to worry about, without being made to feel foolish by having their lack of reason pointed out. Later, when they are well again, they may be curious and may ask. That is the time to tell. If we remember, always, never to do to others what we would not like done to us, then we will not go far wrong. There may be the odd occasion when this rule may be trans-gressed. If so, God will tell us.

People have asked me how I knew such and such was the trouble? The only certain way is by the recovery rate! It is as though you, being ill, go to the doctor. He listens to your account of your symptoms, observes you and then examines you. Then he makes his diagnosis, places you under treatment and you recover. Was it mere chance that you got better, or was it because of his diagnosis and treatment? I guess it could be argued about all night and never proved. The fact remains that you recovered and nothing which had been done previously had brought about the desired result.

Different again was the case of Janice, who was protected and wonderfully cared for but who was reluctant to grow up and had a persistent fear of responsibility. Strange, but true, the 'control' spirit was indolence and it was very difficult to discern. I don't remember how the clue came to me, but I do remember being astonished, as she was one who bustled around, cooking for other members of the family, pressing them to eat. This strange anomaly sometimes seems to be a feature of the malady. In spite of the apparent activity, indolence was at the bottom of it. She liked being spoiled and pampered and enjoyed having things done for her. Part of her was lazy and didn't want to make the necessary effort which responsibility and maturity require.

You will see from these few examples that although the illness had a readily identified syndrome, the reasons behind its onset are so many and varied that it may be said every case is different. To go back to the earlier example of a fort, it is as though either by direct means or by fifth column strategy, a strong attacker gains entry. Under the cover of night, or perhaps in daylight while some distraction is in progress, this attacker unbars and opens various half-hidden doors or windows and lets in his own evil supporters. These, with guile and infamy strive to take over and destroy the fort.

I could write many more tales of those who have suffered anorexia nervosa, but I'll leave it for now. So far, not one of the girls who has come under my care has died and to the best of my knowledge not one has regressed. For this I thank God. It has seemed right to explain about the many and varied reasons so that when you encounter this illness yourselves, you will be cautious and wait for the Spirit to show you things.

You have said that what I have written to you has opened your eyes to endless possibilities as far as intercession is concerned and will be of great help to you in your work and ministry. You can ask me anything, anytime. It is good to have another person to check things out with. The time will come however, when God's voice will speak to you with such clarity that you will know beyond all doubt how you should proceed. Until such time, it is helpful to confer with others if and when you feel the need.

Letter 11

Dear Mark and Sarah

It seems a long time since I wrote to you. So much has been happening but now all is quiet, and I will tell you about Sally, a little girl who screamed.

Sally was, I think, about six years old when her parents got in touch with me through a mutual friend. They had had the child checked over by the family doctor who could find no physical cause for her screaming fits. He proposed psychiatric help if she showed no improvement within a reasonable period of time. This child used to open her mouth and roar, and I do mean **roar**! She would throw herself on the ground emitting such ear-splitting shrieks that parents and onlookers alike became equally perturbed. Nobody could calm her or restrain her. Folk tried everything they knew but no matter what they did she would scream and scream and scream until she was exhausted. Then she would fall asleep where she lay. When she awakened she would not believe that she had done what people told her she had done.

I began to probe and question, and discovered that she never behaved this way in school amongst children of her own age group. It was always in adult company that she screamed. It seemed to be triggered off by the occasions when nobody was taking any notice of her. The first time it happened was when her parents were chatting with friends in the foyer of their church one Sunday morning. It would have been easy to jump to the conclusion that she just wanted to be the centre of attention, but caution said to me, 'Why does being noticed matter so much now, when it didn't seem to matter before? What has happened to change things?'

That night, as I was dropping off to sleep, in a kind of waking dream a scene was enacted for me. I saw a small child in a shop. People were coming and going, collecting milk and papers, magazines and bread – a continuous stream of people. The small one, clutching her money, was crowded out and ignored, unseen by the shop assistant and overlooked by the adult customers. Outside a car waited, and I felt the panic experienced by the little girl. Anyway, I recorded these details before I settled for the night. It always pays to do this, because it is sometimes impossible to recall later, all that one has seen.

I contacted Sally's parents and yes, an incident like this had occurred and it had happened on the afternoon before Sally's very first screaming fit. My excitement rose. This was an example of the Holy Spirit speaking to the mind while the body was in a relaxed state. You have probably had the same thing happen to you. I'm sure that many of us do have experiences like this, but when we remember them we bring our reason to bear on them, decide that they are ridiculous, and dismiss them. If only we would realise that God has other ways of speaking to us besides through reason. If He is the Lord of our whole lives, then can He not speak just as well through emotion, impression, or so-called intuition? I feel that we must get out of the habit of ignoring our 'hunches' because they may be the word of God to us in many situations.

To return to Sally. What had happened was that some relatives were visiting her family and an afternoon drive was in progress. Sally was sent into the shop to buy some ice-creams. Her father remembered his exact words to her when he gave her the money. 'Now don't come back without them and hurry up or we'll go without you.' I suppose that every parent since the year dot has said similar words at some time or other and our children have not ended up screaming like Sally. But to this sensitive little girl it was a fearful situation. If she returned to the car without the goods she would earn the displeasure of both father and uncle and the derision of the visiting cousins. If she waited to be served, they might just go and leave her. Understandable anger arose inside her which only the pressure of circumstances forced her to control. She couldn't control it forever. Adults who pushed her away, walked past her and talked over her head, ignoring her plight and her claims – these were the targets for her bottled rage. Small wonder that it exploded next morning in the church foyer, when her mother and father were chatting to friends.

Anger, panic and fear – these three. Well, I did the intercession. As her life up to then had been reasonably trouble-free, I projected back in time to the incident in the shop, asking Jesus to be there with the child, and believing that He was. I asked that He would notice her distress and would step forward and say to the shop assistant, 'Excuse me, but there is a little girl here waiting to be served.' I built this picture in my mind's eye an claimed, by faith, that the damage which was done to the child at the time would be rectified by the understanding of Our Lord. Her parents cooperated, and avoided potential 'trouble-spots' for a while. Sally never had another screaming fit, whereas she had been troubled by them several times a week for many months before this. It's a lovely story, isn't it?

Her parents were so grateful to God, and to me, as His instrument, and they have become very interested in the disturbances of other children. They have learnt a lot about interceding for them and are also much more sensitive to their own family's needs, becoming much more careful about the words they say to their children.

I have often thought that had I known, years ago, what I know now, my own boys might have had fewer hassles and misunderstandings than they did. It is easy to be wise after the events. I am glad you have asked so much about how to minister to the little ones. I am sure you will be used to prevent or to heal a great deal of unnecessary suffering.

I must stop now as I am expecting a visit from a father with two sick daughters.

Letter 12

Dear Mark and Sarah

So much has happened since last week. The father with the two sick daughters came. His wife was in bed with the flu. The girls are both anorexic but I am sure we will hear good news about them before long. As I was sorting through some papers a few days ago I unearthed a letter which was written some time back, by the father of another girl who had been a victim of the same complaint. It is a lovely letter and I will quote you part of it.

'I never believed in such a thing as an evil spirit until I saw our daughter in the grip of this destructive thing, which my "gut-level" feeling told me was bigger than both of us. My wife and I were in despair, when we heard of you and your ministry. We were like drowning people, clutching at straws. We knew that a loving Creator and a destructive force can have nothing in common. We also believed that the power of God was the stronger. What we did not know was how to use one against the other. This you have taught us. Thank you for your very clear explanation of what was done for Janet. We thank God every day for her recovery. May God richly bless you in your work and your ministry.'

Janet, a beautiful eighteen-year-old had been ill for two years. The onset of her illness was pinpointed well. She had been in a car accident with three other young people, one of whom was fatally injured. The dead girl had been Janet's best friend and it had been Janet herself who had persuaded the lass to accompany her and the two young men, in the car. Janet's appetite left her at the time of the shock. This is what I have now come to call a pyschological disturbance of the eating function. There seemed to be no way she could escape the guilty feeling that she was responsible for her friend's death. The voice in her ear told her that she wasn't fit to live, and her behaviour showed that she had heard the voice and had believed it.

Actually, their car had been crashed into by another vehicle whose driver was drunk, and none of the young people could be held responsible in any way. Janet however, felt guilty. Deception and delusion were dancing together and guilt and fear were following close behind. But the real trouble-maker – the key spirit – was the demon of death, and its job was to destroy life, one way or another.

I asked the Lord to go back in time to the scene of the accident and I re-created that scene in my imagination, with the presence of Jesus there. I asked that He would remedy and reverse the harm that had been done, and thanked Him that the girl who had died was now in His care. Then, after claiming protection for myself, I started the deliverance session.

I spoke to the demon of death and dismissed it into the hands of Jesus – forbidding it – in His Name, to trouble Janet or any other member of her family any more. Then I prayed for the desire to live, to grow in her. As I prayed it came to me that Janet was still grieving for her friend and that when the grief process had been worked through, then the guilty feeling would go. So I asked the Lord to comfort her sorrow, as He has promised to do.

That evening, as I learned later, after having been strangely quiet all day, Janet began to weep, spontan-eously, while she and her family were watching television. Her folk, wisely, made no attempt to stop her or to question her. They just let her cry. She cried most of the night and slept most of the following day. Then she appeared at her mother's elbow, in the kitchen, saying, 'I'd like to cook some scrambled eggs, Mum. I'm hungry.' Mother caught her breath and shed a few tears. It was the first time in two years that Janet had desired food.

So that is Janet's story. I have many more such stories I could tell, but I think that I had better not write any more for a while. It has been wonderful to share with you but life here has been so busy that I cannot spend too much time letter-writing. You know that you can write to me any time if you need to, and also, I feel that perhaps we can continue our correspondence along these lines at a later date. You are bound to come across people in similar kinds of difficulty to those I've told you about in these letters. It was encouraging to hear that much I have written to you about has been a help to you already.

Goodbye for a little while.

PART
TWO

Letter 13

Dear Mark and Sarah

I'm so glad we're in touch again after such a long time. Of course I will answer your questions as well as I can. You must understand that I don't pretend to be an expert. I simply share with people what God has taught me and if they also learn from it that's good. If not, they can leave it on the shelf. God the Holy Spirit has His own way of leading us all, each at his or her own pace, as we become able or willing to absorb different viewpoints or new knowledge.

The first item on your list of requests for information is that of 'curses', which is odd, because the same topic has cropped up time and again in many letters to me over the last year. It is a strange theme to re-start our correspondence with but obviously it needs to be tackled.

What is a curse? How does one pray for or minister to someone who feels that they, or their family, or their children, have been cursed? What do most people mean by it? One's thoughts fly to voodoo, hexes, jinxes or something similar, and while these things do happen, we must not ignore the more subtle forms of cursing. What the words 'under a curse' mean to most people needs to be clarified. We all know that words have power. Words can terrify or persuade, cajole or threaten, build up or break down and on these frequently verifiable observations we base our working definition. Let us say that a curse is 'positive words uttered with power'. Power in this case relating to the degree of effectiveness which transpired.

I knew a lady once, who used to work among prisoners and on one occasion she dealt with a prisoner who, she was sure, was an intelligent young man, but her difficulty lay in getting him to believe it. She enlisted the help of the psychologist and the chaplain and her client reluctantly underwent tests which indicated that his IQ was up in the top bracket and that he was, as she suspected, university material. He simply could not take it in.

'Ever since I started school' he said, 'every teacher always told me I was stupid. Dad and my brothers did too. Dad called me a "no-good useless dreamer" and my brothers said I was stupid because I wasn't like them. Mum died when I was young and they all ganged against me. I cleared out as soon as I could, but I have always been stupid – they all said so!'

My friend's heart ached for this young man. He was not stupid – he was different. He had in effect been cursed. Powerful negative words had been uttered so often and for so long that they became self-fulfilling. The small boy lacked the maturity to negate the words when they were spoken. He simply believed them.

The young man was persuaded to begin a study course and did so well that he surprised himself. If there had been someone to affirm and encourage him when he was little, just as my friend and the chaplain were now doing, he might never have begun a life of crime.

Another meaning of 'to curse' in the dictionary says 'to condemn or assign to hell'. He was assigned to a living hell by his teachers and family.

The scriptures tell us to return cursing with blessing and to pray for those who treat us badly. There are people who think that to do this turns one into a weak doormat. They could not be more mistaken. This is not weakness but strength, and it is not easy to do. In many instances it is amazingly difficult and would be impossible but for the empowering love of Christ. When it is done, one changes from the position of helpless victim, to that of a positive initiator. As such, he or she can no longer be pushed around spiritually, and the curse is broken.

A minister friend and I had dealings with a young mother who was searching for reasons for her son's bad behaviour. He was hostile towards her and his young brother but not towards his father. The hostility went well beyond ordinary sibling rivalry and he also led his mother a merry dance. He needled and baited her constantly but rarely played up when father was within earshot. She investigated all kinds of theories and tried many recommended remedies – none of which was effective.

Eventually she felt guided to explore the family background. Her people came from Scotland and had been involved in fierce border fighting in the old days. Someone's life had been taken and threats had been uttered – along with a heated pronouncement that there would always be 'bad blood' between family members and never any lasting peace in their houses.

After seeing her, we prayed for the boy, and in the name of Jesus, severed any harmful connection between him and his forebears, while asking at the same time that any good link would be fostered and would remain intact. We prayed too for his mother, who had resented him from the moment she knew she was pregnant. For anyone who knew the family circumstances this was understandable, but even so it was wrong and someone had to express regret and ask for forgiveness.

I once told this story at a seminar and a young man said 'Excuse me, but what is the scriptural basis for that?'

Fair question, but didn't Jesus on the Cross pray, 'Father forgive them, they don't know what they do'?

This mother didn't know either, what harm she may have done to her son by resenting the fact that he even existed. Things improved somewhat but she eventually approached the minister again. She had become aware of something inside her which surfaced now and again. We made another appointment for a deliverance session.

She made prayers of confession, spontaneously asking forgiveness for any wrong that her ancestors had done to any other family and asking God to bless the descendants of those who may have been wronged. The minister dismissed a spirit whose name was 'enmity' and I dismissed 'dissention' and 'strife'. She shed some tears and we prayed for her protection in future and said 'thank you' for what she had been able to do. We prayed in faith that from that time forward, there would be nothing but harmony between the blood relatives in the family. You noticed no doubt, that it was mother and brother that the lad reacted against, and not the father or his family. When the mother called to collect her sons from the child-minder after our session together, the certainty that she loved them both, and that she and they were now different, swept over her. And they were, in reality, different. God had changed them and their circumstances.

In this instance the trouble spot lay way back in time. You may remember when I wrote to you before, there was a lady whose female relatives had all died when they were 32 years old and how she was delivered from her fears. Sometimes however, it is much more recent. I know a man who, beginning college in the distant wake of a clever cousin, was told he would never be as good as him, and would probably end up digging ditches. Fortunately he was blessed with greater common-sense and tenacity than most, and he battled his way through that negativity and succeeded in his chosen career. How careful we have to be with our tongues. As the Bible says, 'The tongue is an unruly member.'

So, how do we tell children that certain behaviour is unacceptable without planting negative words in their minds? The key is to condemn the behaviour and not the person. The difference between saying 'you are a bad boy' and 'you have done a bad thing' doesn't seem much but in truth it is enormous. The first phrase eliminates the possibility that he could ever do anything good. The second implies that he is able to choose, but has chosen wrongly this time. It encourages him to make a better choice next time.

Solemn and deliberate ritual 'curses' from cultures other than our own need to be broken – if possible in the hearing of the victim, by someone equally solemn and deliberate who can assert with authority that what he states in the name of Jesus is of supreme power. Cursing involves that which is spoken. Do not be afraid to 'counter-speak' using scripture. If the Son sets us free we are free indeed, and if we behave as though we are still in bondage, then something needs attention somewhere.

I've written enough for now but will continue this theme in my next letter as I have more to tell you.

Letter 14

Dear Mark and Sarah

At last I have few moments to write a little more on the subject of cursing and blessing, the positive and the negative. Or, if you like, the creative and the destructive. When we go back to basics, we find that there are some important principles involved. If we begin at the beginning, in Genesis, we are told that humans were made in the image of God.

In what ways are we like God? We can all think of ways in which we are not like Him, so what characteristics do we share? Early Genesis tells us that, in the beginning, God had some ideas. Let this happen and let that happen. In other words He 'thought', or better still, He 'imagined'. Also we are told that He spoke – He 'said' this and 'said' that. The third thing He did was 'act'. He brought things about – He caused them to happen. These three; imagination, speech and creativity are important ways in which we are like Him. Some members of the animal kingdom have one or more of these characteristics, but only the human race has all three together.

Our ability to speak, particularly, sets us apart from our friends the animals. Bearing this in mind you will see how important it is for us to be careful with our words. I have always felt this way. These feelings were reinforced several years ago by a personal experience.

I was invited to the home of a keen Christian lady, where there was to be a buffet meal, followed by ministry for all and sundry. The ministering couple were visiting from overseas and appeared to be dedicated, able and caring people. They moved around the room laying hands on different people. One lady who received some attention was suffering from a malignant tumour somewhere on her spine. As the gentleman prayed for her, he began to curse the cancer and his wife and the other folk were 'agreeing' with him. Suddenly I felt a jolt as though someone had struck me on the back of the neck. My ear picked up a voice, apparently unheard by anyone else.

'Out of the same mouth ought not to proceed both blessing and cursing – these things ought not to be. Does the same spring yield both fresh and brackish water?'

These words are similar to those found in James 3:10. My initial reaction of shock was followed quickly by an urge to get out of the place and a determination that **nothing** would induce me to allow that man to lay hands on me! The same mouth had produced both blessing and cursing and – for me anyhow – it was not right. (I have never wavered from that position.) I edged towards the door and quietly slipped out feeling a bit bad about not telling anyone why.

Next day my hostess phoned. Had I enjoyed the evening? I related what had happened. 'But it was only the **cancer** that he cursed – not the person.' 'I know that, but it still doesn't make it right.' 'But many people have done it before and cancers **do** shrivel.' 'But I don't remember that Jesus ever did it.' 'But don't forget dear, that Jesus cursed the fig tree.' 'Right, let's look up the story and see why he did.'

There is a brief account in Matthew 21 but the fuller story is told in Mark 11:13, 14 and 20–25. The disciples had seen Jesus heal a blind beggar. They had heard the loud hosannas and had seen Him enter Jerusalem in a triumphal setting. Before that, when James and John had asked for preferential treatment He had said *'You don't understand what you are asking.'* It seems that there were many other things which were not understood either.

The very next day the chance occurred for a practical object lesson – a first-hand demonstration.

> *'On the following day after they had left Bethany, he felt hungry and noticing in the distance a fig tree in leaf, he went to see if he could find anything on it. But when he came there, he found nothing but leaves, for it was not the season for figs. He said to the tree* (while the disciples were listening) *"May no one ever again eat fruit from you."'*

They must have thought 'How odd – why on earth did He say that? He knows it is not fig season yet.'

> *'Early next morning, as they passed by, they saw that the fig tree had withered from the roots up, and Peter, recalling what had happened said to him "Rabbi, look, the fig tree which you cursed* (with powerful negative words) *has withered!"'*

They were seeing, in front of their eyes, the indisputable outcome of those words. Jesus then went on to tell them that **positive** words uttered with power – that is, in faith – will bring positive results. Now isn't this the real lesson that we are to learn from the story? We have it recorded that Jesus told them that even a mountain could be removed into the sea if they were sure that it could happen. We are told elsewhere in Scripture to believe that what we have asked for without doubts will come about. This power – the power of faith – can be used positively or negatively. If we are not going to be destructive we must concentrate on the positive.

Sometimes just straightout prayers for the healing of the past will be effective.

A friend and I ministered to a young man in whom could be seen many talents and great potential, but who never seemed to 'get off the ground'. During our counsel and prayers a curious life pattern emerged. When he was small his older brother bullied him. When he started school the school bully beat him up. Later in life the pattern was repeated time and time again and these negative circumstances began to say something to his inner self.

'You can never take on anything big – you'll get clobbered. If you try you will only get flattened so you'd better not try.'

So he didn't. His own self-image had fallen victim to the negative repetition and although he was intelligent he lacked enterprise and effort.

We prayed that the Lord, who promised to be with us always, would walk back through time and would both comfort and encourage the small boy that he used to be and would make him whole again. We asked that from this time onwards he would have true realisation of his own worth and potential – vision to look ahead with a positive expectation and stamina to see it through. We claimed, in Jesus' name, that these things would now begin to happen. They did! We watched him change as time passed.

Sometimes you may encounter a 'family thing' – Uncle Joe's bad temper or Grandad's stubborness. People can be freed from these things. Sometimes, though, 'it' can skip a generation only to reappear later. I am reminded of a certain family. Grandmother had resented her son's marriage and openly stated that she would break it up. She did not succeed but the two children of the marriage grew up in the shadow of Grandma's resentment, although neither of them appeared to be adversely affected by it to any marked degree. The marriage of the granddaughter began another generation but it was not until **her** two sons were growing up that trouble reared its head. Fierce animosity developed between the boys, so much so that it was not safe to leave them alone together.

In a case like this the pressing need is not so much to deal with the boys as to deal with the past. The parents, the minister and myself counselled and prayed together and a little later I went ahead with what I felt needed to be done. I wrote out my prayer for the whole family. In Jesus' name I severed the harmful link between great-grandmother and great-grandsons asking that all good ties between them would remain intact. I asked for forgiveness for grand-mother, for the damage she had caused and for her poor treatment of her daughter-in-law, her son and his children. I also wrote out a series of less serious incidents connected with the family and asked that the power of the risen Christ would restore harmony in the home and between all the family members. I sealed it up in a self-addressed envelope and placed it on the communion table the following Sunday. Our minister was aware of what I was doing and approved. I retrieved it after the service and sent a copy to the boys' parents. This all happened on 18 November and I have recorded in my diary – 23 January: 'Boys much better. Mother reports she is sure "that thing" is broken.'

Well, we have covered a great deal about curses, haven't we? I've told you about the intentional and the uninten-tional ones – the difference between the deliberate and the casual. Both are destructive, but the latter are less easily identifiable because we tend to have our attention taken by the dramatic but ignore the familiar. We often do not recognise harmful negative words for what they are.

Parents whom I know watched every romance in their daughter's life end in frustration and disappointment. It transpired that she had been told, years before by a fortune-teller at a party, that although her friend would marry, she never would. There was a spirit involved her and I discerned it as 'false prophecy'. The mother and I dismissed it – in absentia – and prayed for the healing of the hurts of the years. Her daughter had, in effect, been cursed, and both deliverance and healing prayers were necessary in order that she might be free.

I also found that I had to pray for forgiveness for the fortune-teller, which was difficult, as the suffering which he had caused this family was enormous, and fortune-tellers are not my favourite people anyhow. The victim's life has undergone transformation. She hasn't married yet, but she could if she chose! She is lovely, caring, integrated and whole.

You meet many people who can tell you just what is wrong in any given situation. If you ask them what they have done about it they give you a blank stare. It has not occurred to them to do anything. I tell these folk, 'If you can discern, you are obliged to pray.' Pray that the opposite state of affairs begins to come about. This kind of ministry is something which any believing Christian with half a grain of faith can do for anybody else. We know that the Creator brought order out of chaos and if we do the same thing we are in line with His intention, aren't we? This whole attitude of reversing the negative, whenever we come across it, not only benefits the victims but is good for us, too. It trains us by repetition to build up instead of breaking down. It means that although we can see the faults and failings in others, we can begin to imagine that person without them, and pray in faith this might come about. Let us never forget that we are the channels through which God's power flows in order to restore the world.

Letter 15

Dear Mark and Sarah

I promised that I would write to you about dreams and at last I have a little time to do so. You have asked if you should take any notice of them, and my reply is that you can't help but take notice. What sort of notice however, is what we need to decide. I suspect that your real question is whether God really does guide us or speak to us through or in our dreams.

We all dream, the experts tell us, whether we are aware of it or not. Some vivid episodes we remember – others fade from us. Allowing for the fact that various stresses of life, or what we ate or drank at dinner time, or that issues concerning work, play or our innermost thoughts may all have a bearing on what we dream, we are still left with much evidence pointing towards the conclusion that there are times when we are guided in this way. It is as though one's 'inner self' speaks to one's 'outer self' about things which may not have become known otherwise and if God has first spoken to that 'inner self' – spirit to spirit – then we are in business.

Often we dream in pictures and/or symbols and the code has to be cracked before the message becomes clear. Remember in one of our conversations I told you about a lad who repeatedly dreamed that he was in a dark, spooky place and was torn between the urge to touch a crystal ball, and another urge not to? I used this case history during several workshops and was amazed to find that almost without exception, people jumped to the conclusion that he'd been dabbling in the occult. Nothing could have been further from the truth. Because I knew that he was an adopted boy, I realised immediately that the crystal ball was a symbol of the unknown. On arriving at adolescence he had a momentous and far-reaching decision to make. Should he enquire into the past to discover his natural parents or not? To touch the unknown or not to touch? That is typical of a person's inner questionings surfacing during sleep. He wondered why he'd never dreamed it in previous years and the answer to that was simple too – he was not ready to handle it earlier on and neither was it an issue for him then.

You will see that everything connected with our dreams has to be put through the sieve of our commonsense when we awaken, as it is largely the logical, reasonable and critical faculties which are suspended while we are dreaming. Where else but in a dream do we fly like a bird, fall over a cliff and bounce, or turn purple when we eat birthday cake?

The mother of a young family came to me once, unsettled and puzzled. She had had a rotten dream, and very vivid and unforgettable it was, too. She dreamed that she lay in a hospital bed on life support – dying of cancer. One part of her said, 'Might as well just let go and drift off,' and the other half said, 'I can't die yet God, I've got a husband to care for and a family to bring up.' She was left in a disturbed state of mind. Was she going to get cancer and die? It is seldom that such a dream becomes literally true, but we'll talk about that later. Allowing for the possibility that the whole thing was probably symbolic, my first question to her was, 'What's eating you?'

It seemed to me that there must be something waiting to be resolved which was gnawing away inside of her. It transpired that she was unhappy in her job. She worked in an old people's home and had caught herself many times reacting negatively against the constant complaints and self-centredness of some of the patients. But what should she do? She needed the money. I felt it quite in order to pray, as it was obvious that a different environment would be beneficial – that the opportunity for a change in occupation would be open for her – and it did!

Now to get back to the warning dreams. The Bible has many such accounts. The wise men were warned in a dream not to return to Herod. Joseph was warned in a dream to take the infant Jesus and his mother and go to Egypt. I have listened to folk many times who, when a dream with dire results came their way, lived in fear and trembling expecting the calamity to inescapably eventuate.

Now if you are travelling along the road in your car and another vehicle weaves towards you out of control, you take evasive action. And if you take evasive action and attempt to avoid some calamity when something 'comes at you' in space, why not take similar evasive action when something may be coming at you in time? You have been given a preview, if you like, of a possible (not an inevitable) outcome of certain sets of events – not that you should fatalistically expect disaster but in order that you might take steps to avoid it. Think about it.

I had a warning dream once. Some years ago I awoke in the early hours of the morning with a ghastly pain in my lower spine. I felt as though I had been hit in the back with a sledge-hammer and the jolt of agony woke me up. I'd been dreaming. I was walking down a corridor. People were coming and going. Glass panelled swing-doors with shiny metal handles were being swung to and fro by the passing crowds. I pushed my door one way and pushing the door the other way were a young couple – a girl with long brown hair and a young man in a duffle coat with toggle buttons. It was their door, swinging back as they passed, which jolted my spine and caused such pain.

Later that day I was part of the exiting throng pouring out of a lecture room in the University. There, across the corridor, were the identical doors and coming towards me –

would you believe – were a young man in a duffle coat and a girl with long brown hair! I stepped aside smartly and stayed by the wall until they had passed.

My dream had been sent to warn me. I had taken evasive action and had been kept from harm. I was deeply grateful and strangely happy inside. I had been 'warned by God in a dream'.

The dreams that we remember may be the surfacing of interior conflict or indecision needing to be worked through, or a picture of a possible, but not inevitable, outcome of circumstances – they may be in a 'code' and likely to be presented symbolically. They can speak to us, inspire us, sometimes guide us and at other times warn us, but let us not forget that good old solid quality – common-sense. We do need to be careful to distinguish the vivid, memorable and persistent dream from the fleeting and rambling outworking of yesterday's petty upheavals as our brains unscramble, while we sleep, that which we failed to work through in our waking hours.

Children's nightmares are different and can be very, very distressing not only for the poor child, but also for the whole family. The basis is nearly always unresolved fear. A young mother came to see me once. Her eight year old son had been plagued by nightmares several times a week since he was six. They had no idea what triggered them, but the whole household became more and more tense and the other family members came to dread them as much as he did. He fought against going to sleep as sleep held terrors. A physical checkup produced nothing of note and my ministry was suggested.

I interviewed the mother, made some notes, chatted to our minister and we prayed. We worked through the lad's past, in absentia, in much the same way as I outlined in my first letter to you. We felt that there could be some spiritual interference and his mother remembered an incident which she felt was significant. The lad had been watching an approved TV programme and while mother was otherwise occupied and unaware of the time, another programme began. It was 'The Incredible Hulk'. When we came to this incident during our prayers I had a mental picture of his fears. They looked like 'hungry enzymes' only black, and with legs. There were five of them and as I began to dismiss them, they spread out from their cluster and began to scatter.

I remember saying out loud, 'Don't you dare part company!' and they joined hands again! We dismissed them all, as a group, and asked that the peace of God would fill the gaps left by their departure.

That was the end of the nightmares. He had a few disturbed and wakeful nights as both body and mind had become used to a roller-coaster sleep pattern, and his whole system had to learn afresh what an uninterrupted night was. But there were no more fears. I saw the lad a fortnight later and he looked so different it was incredible. He has never looked back.

A young father whom I knew was equally concerned about his young daughter. She had shocking nightmares. None of the other children had ever been troubled in this way. They tried everything. It was nothing physical, not anything psychological that they could discover. One night this Dad had a sudden certainty that it was a spirit at work. He was angry. They were committed Christians and had prayed over and over again for the child. This time was different.

He stood in the middle of the living room – to all intents and purposes addressing thin air – and he exploded.

'You spirit of fear,' he said, 'just what do you think you are doing in my house, frightening my child? You get to hell out of here – do you hear me? And don't you dare come back, ever again. This house belongs to Jesus and so do we and in His name I tell you to clear out!'

Not exactly the most churchy of phraseology but so what? Sometimes I feel that people mimic words which they have heard others use and which they have not really made their own. The words should express a principle in which we believe and are not in themselves a magical formula.

This father recognised the enemy at work, believed utterly in the victory of the risen Christ over evil in any form, and articulated his belief in his own way and with authority.

They all slept like babies that night. The child never had another nightmare. Then the father wondered 'Why did the spirit never go when we prayed? Why did it only go when I ordered it?'

That brings us to the next request on my list from you – 'Can you teach us more about evil and how to handle it?' Well, that is a tall order, but I'll write about that the next time.

Letter 16

Dear Mark and Sarah

Your earlier request for some basic information about 'evil' has coincided with the incident that I wrote about last time concerning the young father and his little daughter, who was troubled by nightmares.

This was the dilemma which the parents had to work through – why didn't the fear go when they had prayed 'hundreds of times' that God would deal with it? It only went when the father spoke to it and ordered it out of the house.

Perhaps we should go back to basics. I don't expect you to accept all I say uncritically. There is too much of that going on in the world already. You need to probe and question and check things out with what is in scripture. Nobody would argue that there is no evil in the world, except perhaps, those who like to think it is simply the absence of good. We are all aware of suffering and sorrow, pain and pathos, anger and agony. And sometimes, an odd amalgam of happiness and high spots. The Bible tells us that this chaotic state was brought about by human disobedience. Broadly speaking, it speaks of two kinds of evil:

1. That which is part of our human nature because we are sinful people, and
2. That which is not part of us but which has infiltrated body, mind and/or personality, from outside of ourselves.

The remedy for human sin is repentance, confession, acceptance of forgiveness, prayer, effort and discipline. Jesus died in order that we might be forgiven and have a restored relationship with our Father.

The remedy for invading evil is eviction. It must be thrown out, told to go, dismissed or whatever phraseology you are familiar with. It is not the phrases, but faith in the principle which is important. Jesus rose from the dead in order that victory over evil might be complete, and so it is, but in order for it to be effective in the world around us, we have to appropriate it, both on our own and on behalf of others.

Just as not everybody has accepted Jesus' victory over sin (on the Cross), neither has everybody accepted the victory over evil brought about by His resurrection. Everybody may – but not everybody will. We have a choice.

Now you can see what the young couple in the story were doing. To begin with, they were applying the wrong remedy and what happened to them on a small scale has happened to many thousands of Christians in umpteen branches of the Church down the ages.

Many dear, devout and devoted people have struggled and struggled against evil in their lives or the lives of families and friends, when there was no way that it would budge until somebody ordered it to leave in the name of Jesus.

Conversely, there are branches of the church who have 'majored' in deliverance ministry and have blamed anything and everything on to the devil, or Satan, or his servants, demons or evil spirits, leaving no room for human choice, human disobedience, and/or human error. In such circles the devil is the chief topic of conversation and his latest 'attacks' are occasions for comment. The attitude is at times the perfect cop-out.

These folk have been applying the second remedy as a universal panacea for all ills, when a little self-discipline and obedience to the scriptures would have provided lasting improvement in many instances. You will no doubt see, as I have come to see, that the real truth lies in finding a balance between these extremes, being aware of all possibilities, rubbishing none, and taking great care with diagnosis before we flash hasty 'discernments' around or wound another person by our too speedy judgements or unthinking comments. If I have been forthright and outspoken about the topic it is because I have seen so much suffering caused through failure to perceive which is the correct course of action to take.

I once had a lady say to me 'I'm sure my family has been cursed,' and because I knew so much about their background and their deliberate wayward conduct, in all honesty I had to say to her, 'I'm sorry my dear, but your family members have brought most of their troubles on their own heads. They are reaping what they have sown. They knew that what they were doing was wrong and yet they have persisted and chosen to continue.'

Strictly speaking we don't break the laws of God – we rebel against them and they break us! If I walk off the edge of a cliff I have not broken the law of gravity. I have rebelled against it and it has broken me. Far better not to walk in that direction in the first place. I sometimes think that if folk could even see the ten commandments as a set of warning notices, instead of a set of punishable prohibitions, how much better off we would be. It is as though God says, 'My dear children, the ideal society that I planned for you will only run one way – if you try other ways you'll only get hurt, so please don't try.'

You will see then, that part of the minister's or counsellor's skill must be in becoming aware, one way or another, of which kind of evil we are dealing with, and which treatment is appropriate. I have sometimes heard with dismay of some kindly-intentioned person who has leapt to the fore and 'cast out' a spirit of confusion or doubt or whatever, when what the person really needed was time and help to work through their doubts and confusion, soaking up the word of God until they'd stake their life on the promises contained there. I'm not saying that confusion and/or doubt are never caused by spirits, but what I am saying is – let's make haste slowly and at all times act in love, which means acting for the person's ultimate well-being.

I've known folk who very much wanted to get rid of certain troublesome things but who had no intention of changing their ways or adapting their lifestyle. I remember being with a minister friend at one time and two teenage girls arrived to see him. They had been to a séance and one of them had been taken over by another entity and had – as she put it – really freaked out.

They had no church background at all but seemed to know that you had to 'fight fire with fire'. One lass had to leave and her spooked friend remained to be counselled. The minister carefully explained how she had endangered herself spiritually by attending the séance and that she'd had evidence that the procedure had been harmful to her. She was terrified of being 'taken over' again. He explained about Jesus and His power over everything in the spirit world and that yes, we could minister to her in His name and that she would be free – both of 'the thing' and her own fears – but first she needed to resolve never to be a part of any occult practice ever again.

She sat in silence, and so did we. We sat and sat. Then she spoke and I shall never forget her reply. 'Well I could give up going to the séances but I don't see anything wrong with a ouija board!' She had made her choice and under the circumstances neither the minister nor I felt that it was wise to proceed until such time as she changed it.

There are many people who say they don't believe in evil spirits. They tend to discount the evidence because of the imagery. Give them a different image and their whole outlook changes. One of the better definitions is, perhaps, 'a force motivating a person towards his own or another's destruction'. A Christian can never be completely owned by any other power but he can be afflicted or troubled by a destructive force, and it is our job, as disciples, to learn about evil and how to handle it when it rears its head.

These days there is much literature available on this subject, and although most of it is helpful, one still has to avoid falling into the trap of mouthing the words of a formula that one has heard someone else use. We need to be sure, in our own minds, of the principle upon which our words and actions rest and the best way, I believe, is to study the instances of deliverance ministry which are recorded in the gospels and simply update the language so that it is easily understood.

I shall write more about that next time but wanted to finish today's letter by telling you a personal story from the past about how I became involved in this kind of ministry in the early days.

I was on a long journey to visit some friends when suddenly a man, driving extremely carelessly, overtook us at a dangerous place where his visibility must have been nil! I remarked that he would be off the road if he wasn't careful. Sure enough, we hadn't gone much further when we saw that he had run off the road and his vehicle now lay – wheels up – in a ditch. He was not injured and was arrogantly ordering a passing motorist to take him to the nearest garage to get assistance. The other occupants of the other vehicle involved were both shaken and it was obvious, from the placement of their car and the tyre marks, that the careless one had hit them and spun their vehicle around. They were clearly the 'innocent parties'.

The old gentleman was pale, quiet and a bit dazed. The lady was a different kettle of fish. She sat on the roadside bank showing all the signs of a fine case of screaming hysteria. I attempted to do what I could for her, but nothing – not even a resounding slap – relieved the situation. Her words about her husband and his driving were both wild and stupid, as anyone could see that the accident had not been his fault. I could see that she was in the grip of something beyond her control. In a flash I knew what it was and anger swept over me. In fact, I was so angry that I acted instinctively. I put my hand on her shoulder and said, 'You – spirit of panic – how dare you show yourself through this woman! You have no business here. In the name of Jesus I tell you to go away, this minute – do you hear me? Get out!'

The effect was dramatic. She stopped yelling, shook her head from side to side, clapped a hand over her mouth and said 'Whatever have I been saying dear? I just don't know what got into me.' 'Well I know what got into you,' I replied, 'you've had a panic fit. I expect the shock caused it.'

'Thank goodness you knew what to do dear,' she said, 'thank you so much. I'm sure I'll be alright now.'

Little did she know that I'd had no idea what to do! I got thrown in at the deep end. I had no training neither had I read any literature. I'd never even thought much about evil spirits, but along with everyone else, I'd read the Bible stories and when the necessity arose they had formed the pattern along which I acted. Why should people suffer in the grip of these things when they can be set free?

Letter 17

Dear Mark and Sarah

At last I have a few moments to write to you. I'm glad my last letter to you was just what you needed to know. As I haven't finished yet, let's continue.

If we return to my story about the lady with the 'panic' several questions arise. The first one is 'How did I know what the spirit was?' On that particular occasion I can only say that God told me. Frequently we do become aware intuitively of the root of a particular trouble, but this is not always the case. On other occasions we must observe behaviour, and the symptoms which we see appearing time and again give us an overall picture, enabling us to label the entity.

So there are at least two well-known methods of discovery:
1. Discernment and
2. Detection

When one works a lot with children as I have done over the years, observation of behaviour is crucial. Small children can't tell – their vocabularies are inadequate anyway – and the intercessor is given reports from parents, teachers, friends, and especially grannies. Grannies are marvellous. Life has, no doubt, given them an eye for the unusual and a nose for the other than normal.

It is much easier in any kind of deliverance ministry, if you know the name of the entity involved. Instead of the

Dear Mark and Sarah...

problem being a huge unknown mass of something bad
'out there' it is a set of symptoms or a repeated behaviour
pattern which is so distinctive that it has a personality of
its own. If it is defined and named, it is brought down to
size and becomes a target for us to exercise our faith
against. I believed that the panic would leave the lady
because I ordered it to go, in the name of Jesus. It never
crossed my mind to doubt – everything happened too
quickly anyway. This brings us to a very important place
and I'm going to make a very important statement. When
you have identified an evil spirit, if **you treat it like an
entity it will behave like an entity**.

Now let's tackle the area of power and authority. In the
gospels we are told that when Jesus sent His disciples out
He gave them *'power and authority over every kind of evil.'*
Read Luke 9:1 and 10:1, 17. Remember the story too, of the
person who was 'casting out evil spirits' in the name of
Jesus and the disciples who overheard objected because he
wasn't one of them. What he did was effective though. He
believed it would be. Jesus' reply on that occasion was to
leave him alone – *'he who is not against us, is for us!'*

In our English language we tend to lump 'power' and
'authority' together as though they were two words meaning the same thing but this is not the case in the Greek.
The two words stem from different roots and, as most of us
are not expert Greek scholars, I sometimes use this simple
illustration to clarify the situation.

I have a friend in the Traffic police. Imagine a three-ton
truck fully loaded and hurtling down a hill on the high-
way. If my friend stepped out into the path of the
oncoming truck in his street clothes, waving wildly at
the driver, he would be likely to get a blast from the horn
and a lot of cursing from the driver.

If, however, he stepped out wearing his full uniform it
would be a different story. The truck would come to a
standstill. The officer does not have the physical force, or
power, to stop the truck. What he has got is the authority
from a body much greater than he, which has empowered

him. In this case it is the full force of the law. When we use the name of Jesus we are bringing His authority to bear on the situation. Let us never forget that. His is the Name which is above every name and we do well to remember it often. Let us never become sloppy in our thinking and imagine that because we have come to know Jesus as Saviour and friend that He has suddenly ceased to be Lord!

I have known well-intentioned people who have run into great trouble because they thought they had God in their pockets and had begun to tell Him what He ought to be doing. I've even heard prayers to this effect. Such prayers, it appears, are supposed to be exhibiting great faith and confidence, but the usually come across as colossal cheek. Something is unbalanced somewhere if people, as they emphasise God's love, forget to also emphasise His majesty.

I have digressed. To return to the lady with the panic. The questions are raised. 'How do these evil entities gain a foothold in someone's life? How is it that they can afflict people as they do, and how do they get in?'

In the case of our lady, her resistance was lowered by shock. Just as we, in a physical sense, although normally healthy, can pick up a virus or flu bug when our resistance is lowered, so it can also be in the spiritual sense. Just as we try to maintain physical health, so we should also try to maintain spiritual health. If however, we do become sick, let us try to regain health as soon as possible. Some of the observed ways in which evil invades are:

1. Shock – accident, illness, grief and/or emotional trauma.
2. Over-indulgence in normal appetites e.g. food, drink, sex.
3. Invitation – usually through occult practises, various forms of spiritism or psychic activity.

Unlike 1, with 2 and 3 there is an element of choice involved. Occasionally there may be something carried over from the past but I may deal with that another time. Nearly always, with children, shock is the key. Children are stunned and left vulnerable by such things as minor surgery, anaesthetic, death of a family pet, break up of a marriage, bullying by an older child, sexual molestation, the death of a grandparent, unjust punishment, cot death of a baby who had been looked forward to. If we train ourselves to watch for these incidents we can often diagnose the trouble.

I once had dealings with a young woman called Catherine. She was a 'Lifeline' counsellor and while manning the phone one Sunday afternoon she answered a call from a woman who had, ostensibly phoned to discuss a problem. Before long however, she was telling Catherine things about herself that she had no legitimate means of knowing. She described Catherine – her size, colouring, the dress she was wearing, what her husband looked like and how many children she had. It was weird. Catherine kept her wits and skilfully terminated the call, but she was very upset. With great courage she held out until it was time to go home and under great stress, weeping and feeling dreadful, she managed to drive to her friend's house. Between tears and breathlessness her friend pieced the story together, put Catherine in her car and drove her to church. Our minister was occupied so I attended to her in the chapel. Her friend had related to me what was known of the circumstances. I said 'We are dealing with something evil here, Catherine, and I will attend to it in a minute. Firstly I feel that I need to pray for myself,' which I did – a simple prayer for guidance and God's care for me in the situation.

Catherine was distraught and breathless. 'Some thing is having a go at you,' I said, 'and the link is the lady caller – we have to sever it.' So I simply stated, 'In the name of Jesus I now sever any harmful link between Catherine and her caller, and I say that the one shall affect the other no more.' I continued 'You, spirit of divination, your presence is discovered – you have no right to be troubling Catherine. In Jesus' name I tell you to go and never come back.' Catherine, although exhausted, began to breathe more normally. The spirit had tried to control her and had failed. Fleetingly, she had wondered if there could be anything in this psychic business, because of the woman's personal knowledge of her affairs. She had resisted as best she could but had been badly frightened. My prayer for guidance was important, because it made sense to 'sever the link' before dismissing the spirit.

The prerequisite for dealing with evil in this manner is supreme confidence in the superiority of Jesus over every other force in heaven and earth and over every other spirit, evil or benign. Jesus is Lord, full stop! One of the old ideas – still present among some folk is the that of 'dualism'. Broadly speaking the definition is that God and the devil are in opposite corners of a gigantic boxing ring waiting for the bell to ring for the next round. It's anyone's guess who will win as the two opponents are so evenly matched. Such suppositions are untenable. The Christian does not entertain dualistic theory. Jesus is Lord. The outcome of the bout is a foregone conclusion and although the 'opposition' may appear to win the odd skirmish, the long-term result is never in doubt.

So our attitude here must be similar to that of the person with the curses, who, by returning blessing for cursing, retains his certainty of ultimate victory and changes his stance from 'victim' to 'initiator'. The one who has to deal with evil, by his confidence in the promises of scripture, changes his stance from that of a battler against evil on God's behalf, to that of a victor against evil because he is empowered by God's Spirit. The circumstances may be almost identical – indeed, I have seen people smitten by parallel circumstances – one was living in victory while the other was forever battling with the possibility of defeat.

One's attitude of mind should always presume superiority over evil in the power of the Holy Spirit and there's nothing like a solid grounding in scripture to maintain that attitude.

I really must bring this to a close but before I do, will you read through say, Luke's gospel and make notes of each recorded instance of deliverance ministry. You, who have seen and heard people minister in this way, will be amazed at what is **not** in the gospels! Many phrases and practices in current usage are simply not there!

You will find no instance of 'binding hand and foot'. After all, how can something be told to go if it is bound hand and foot? How can it possibly move?

See how important our words are? You won't find the phrase 'we come against this and that' or 'we stand against this or that.' If you have an attitude of battle then battle is what you'll get. We are not here to struggle against evil spirits – we are here to forbid them to manifest on this earth and afflict people. In dealing with evil we do not wield power – we wield authority. Power lies in Jesus. He has already won the battle.

Another thing you will not find any reference to is the blood of Jesus. Jesus gave authority over evil and power to heal disease to the twelve and later to the seventy, before He went to the Cross and before His blood was shed. Admittedly, spirits do not like to hear about the Blood because it was shed for the salvation of the human race and they don't want us to be 'saved'. They will often leave rather than hear about it, but they leave by their own choice and not because of your order in the name of Jesus. I have come to see that it is unwise to give them that choice, so I do not use the phrase. I am not telling you what you ought or ought not to do. I'm saying do your own research – this is what I discovered and perhaps you will find the same. I only ever share what God has taught me and I do not personally criticise anyone else. I just make plain the reasons for my own conduct.

I pray that you will both be guided into all truth, and hope that what I have written will be helpful.

Letter 18

Dear Mark and Sarah

When you asked 'Will you write to us about depression, and how we can help if and when it strikes someone we know?' my heart went thump! One could write a whole book and still leave out something vital. I'll begin with a story about Lorna, an attractive young mother. She had a wonderfully understanding husband, two little girls, no financial worries, an expensive home – but she was depressed. Every day was a drag. The struggle she had to cope with just elementary housekeeping jobs was incredible. She had sought assistance and had been sent to a clinic, attendance at which involved driving to town and back on a regular basis. She managed it with great effort but had an almost irresistible urge to drive straight into the pylons which supported the motorway over-bridges. It was all she could do to keep the car on the road.

Life was a black hole. Various people tried to help but patience would wear thin when the situation failed to improve. Then remarks would be made. 'It's about time she snapped out of it,' or 'She doesn't do anything to help herself,' or 'She's just neurotic,' – how I dislike that smug, unfeeling phrase. I went to see her one day. She sat on the floor in the middle of the luxurious shagpile carpet in the living room, in floods of tears. 'What's wrong with me?'

she asked. 'Why am I like this? I've got everything but I've got nothing.'

I offered what support I could, promising two things – that she could phone me any hour day or night, if need be, and that the minister and myself would pray. Not about her depression, but about its cause – or causes.

We duly did and it was not long afterwards that I had a growing conviction that it had something to do with chemical imbalance and I said so.

Meanwhile events began to unfold. She was advised to go into a psychiatric hospital for assessment and she agreed to go. Many people reacted negatively. 'Oh, how terrible. Why haven't our prayers been answered? Why doesn't God **do** something?'

God was 'doing something' but they failed to perceive Him in action, working through ordinary channels. At the hospital she underwent many tests and it was discovered that the sodium-potassium balance in her system was out of kilter. She was taken off sodium salt and was given a potassium substitute and was put on medication suitable for her condition.

Within a few days there was improvement. Within a few weeks she was a new person. Within three months she not only ran her home and looked after her children efficiently, but she started a part-time job. Such changes – in a girl who was terrified of a bridge pylon!

There are several important things to note in this story and much that we can learn. I wonder how the critics felt. Were they at all regretful that they had jumped to hasty conclusions, had failed to give Lorna the benefit of the doubt, had labelled the poor girl neurotic, had expected her to pull herself together and out of the mire, and most importantly, had failed to see God at work through ortho-dox channels? I had been alerted to the fact that the cause involved chemical imbalance but all I could do was pray that God would guide those who were testing her and that the right treatment would be given and that the long-term result would be good.

On another occasion a friend sent a young missionary nurse to see me for counselling. She was a beautiful girl and when she began to tell me about her feelings she burst into tears. She wept her way through the entire afternoon. The main problem was not her depression, it was her guilt. Missionary nurses were not supposed to get depressed. They were expected to work in unbelievable conditions and emerge triumphant over every difficulty. After all, if they were doing the Lord's work, then surely the Lord would supply the necessary resources and if it became obvious that those resources were running down a little then there must be something wrong with the spiritual side of the person concerned. You wouldn't credit how cruel people can be to each other, not so much by what is said, as by what they leave unsaid, but imply. She felt that it was all her own fault, that she had let everybody down, and that she was a complete and utter failure.

It transpired, when she had had a complete medical, that her blood was a veritable menagerie of bugs. Hepatitis, dengue fever, you name it – she'd had it. Within a few weeks she was transformed. 'Things began to come right,' she reported back to me, 'the day you heard me out and let me cry and accepted me as I was.'

There are many lessons to be learned from this story too. I got so that I would not undertake to counsel anyone with depression, until and unless they had had a complete medical check-up. I don't do so much counselling these days but when I do I still tend to look to the 'physical' first. Maybe we lack some mineral or vitamin or eat too much food that's been tinkered and tampered with. A short course of multi-vitamins never seems to go amiss and may have quite a revealing outcome.

Having regard always to possible causes of depression, what about mental and spiritual aspects? Many women have decided they are going mad, or that life is just not worth living, only to discover that some hormonal imbalance was the culprit. There are, though, several causes of depression which crop up time and again – like pessimism, self-pity, guilt, resentment and anger. Have you heard that 'depression is anger turned inward'? A bit of a sweeping statement perhaps, but one with some truth in it.

Some people have a life full of disappointments and arrive at middle-age with a permanent sinking feeling. I remember one lady, Mary, who discovered on her honeymoon, that her husband had deceived her about certain aspects of his life. She was stunned but determined to make the best of things. After all, she did love him and had promised 'for better or worse'.

Three children later, life was busy and interesting. She spent her time caring, encouraging, educating, planning, balancing the budget, providing the children with the best food, clothing, education, entertainment and sporting and cultural opportunities which were available at the time. They accepted it all as their right and expected more. One by one they reappeared on the doorstep, in debt, in strife, in trouble. More money, time and effort were spent on them. One by one they abused her for running out of money, time and effort. Then she discovered that her husband blamed her for the way each of their children had turned out. A black cloud oppressed her. Her fiftieth birthday arrived – which neither husband nor family bothered to remember – and she took stock of her life. The past was black. The present was black. The future was black. What was there to live for? She swallowed pills.

The hospital staff fought for her life but what could they do for her wounded spirit? A friend emerged from out of the mist, a neighbour named Anne, who had herself struggled out from under the black cloud some years before. Slowly and carefully she walked the long road back to recovery with Mary, who eventually became able to make decisions again.

For anyone who sincerely wants to help such people, it is worthwhile to enrol for a counselling course. We need practical skills and information about what to do – and what not to do! As Christians, we have the vast resources of a loving God available through prayer but we need to learn how to channel 'the power'. Do we pray **with** depressed people, or **for** them, or both?

I have known of instances where a service of laying on of hands has brought an injection of new life to the depressed person, resulting in a lasting cure and in a completely transformed life. At other times it has appeared that no change occurred. We must be guided at the time. Each person is unique and so are their needs.

Sometimes deliverance ministry is necessary, but even when spirits have been dismissed, the reasons why they were there and loopholes where they gained access must be attended to if the person is to remain whole. Take self-pity as an example. Why does anyone sink into a state of being permanently sorry for themselves? The door is opened the first time they harbour a grudge, feel aggrieved and let it smoulder, envy someone else's good fortune or fail to be thankful for their own.

Each time they fail to forgive, persist in resentment, wallow in negativism and continually criticise destruct-ively, they are issuing a standing invitation to the spirit to come and live inside them and colour their lives. Is it any wonder that it shifts in, takes up residence and thinks that it owns the house? When the scriptures tell us to be thankful in all things and to form the habit of praise, we ought to take notice.

The Bible says that if we have a difference with someone we should try to sort it out. If it works, we've got some-where – if it doesn't, at least we've tried, and then it becomes the other person's problem. We're also told not to let the sun go down on our wrath but I have met people who have let 365×60 suns go down and are still wrathful, having lived an entire life in anger. We really do become what we habitually think and do.

These scriptural bits of advice are not pious platitudes but a recipe for constructive living. To obey or not to obey? That is the question. Some folk have no intention of obeying but they still want the constructive life. Recently I spoke to a nursing sister. She has seen many patients who have had by-pass heart surgery. Some go home. They stop smoking, they stop drinking. They follow professional advice about food. Others go home. They continue to smoke. They continue to drink. They ignore dietary advice. In five years time those who have survived that long are back, expecting another by-pass.

The stories I have told you so far have concerned women but many of our men have their troubles too. Stresses, fears and disappointments of life still take their toll. They fear loss of income, loss of health, inability to succeed. Their families disappoint them. They slave to provide children with opportunities they never had, only to encounter ingratitude. They flog themselves physically to stay on top or gain promotion, with the spectres of many that are younger and brighter waiting in the wings to take their places. If there is marital strife or unhappiness the problems are compounded. Many of our men folk suffer intensely, often suppressing their emotions to danger point because 'big boys don't cry'.

We like to think we are reasonable human beings, but very few of us act reasonably. When reason and emotion are in conflict, emotion will dictate both action and reaction most of the time. What we feel is usually what motivates us. If we would only stop and think, very often we would behave differently.

Often we don't realise that as well as disobedience in what we do, say or think, we can include our failure to reach full potential. Most of the troubles which we have in life seem to stem either from our own sin, or our reactions to the sins of others. Often, prayers for memory healing, or inner healing bring about startling changes, especially in the self-esteem level.

I could write much more but I feel I've said enough to warn you of some pitfalls and also give you some ideas about what to look for when depression appears in folk with whom you come in contact. Watch out too, for drug involvement of any kind and don't overlook the possibility of occult influence. Also, if there has been a bereavement in the family, a certain amount of 'depression' for a certain length of time is to be expected and should be worked through in the person's own time. This of course, will vary enormously.

Letter 19

Dear Mark and Sarah

By now you will have received the letter about depression. Since writing it I have felt that I left something out which I believe may be important to you in the future – the question of young people and depression. Perhaps we ought to consider it before I get on to the next topic. One hears various remarks. Some say young people have never had it so good. Others decide they wouldn't like to be growing up in today's world with all it's pressures. Where does the truth lie?

It is true that – in our country at least – most young folk have certain advantages not shared by the youth of many other countries. It is also true that privilege brings with it responsibility, subjecting our young folk to pressures which the older generation often fail to appreciate. Because the competitive urge is fostered at a very young age and success in sport, education etc. is seen as something supremely commendable, our young people have a spectre stalking their every step – relentlessly pushing and driving. It is the **fear of failure**.

There is not much room at the top. A large percentage are not going to make it, and they know it. Apart from localised circumstances and the tensions associated with them, there are also the global fears. What is happening to the planet? What about pollution – radioactivity – toxic chemicals – the nuclear issue? Now we have more threats. The 'greenhouse' effect and the ozone layer. What does the future hold? What is the use of striving if some clown is going to push the button and blow us all into oblivion?

Some years ago, I had some dealing with a young man. He lay on his living room floor. Beautiful sunshine was flooding in, his stomach was full, his prospects were rosy and his family loved him – but his mind was troubled and his mood was black. He stared at the ceiling, despair written all over him. With great difficulty he croaked 'Can you tell me why the hell we are on the earth?'

After a short conversation I said, 'Yes, I can tell you. You are not going to like it, neither are you going to believe it but I'm going to say it anyway and you're going to remember it. You are on this earth to learn how to love – under all sorts of conditions. This life is an interlude – a most important and valuable interlude. It's the only learning time you've got. If we don't learn how to love while we have the chance, how are we ever going to feel "at home" in the presence of God – who is love?'

He didn't appear to like it, believe it, accept it or even remember it for very long but I was astonished, years later, to discover that a younger brother, who had overheard the interchange, had remembered it for a very long time indeed. We never know, do we?

If you have dealings with depressed young people, take them seriously. Listen to them and get some expert help for them. Our suicide rate is too high already. I mentioned physical reasons in my last letter. Because of their rapid growth and burgeoning maturity, few of them give much thought to their own health. They will exercise frantically but will fill up their frames with all manner of junk food. Combined with late nights it is, in itself, a killer.

It is impossible, in a letter like this, to do anything else but generalise. The reasons behind teenage depression are many and varied. Just remember to listen and take them seriously. They have their lives ahead of them. Let us pray that they become whole people who can learn to love.

Your next question is about adopted children. 'Why do so many of them seem to be such a handful?' We all know that there are many thousands of adopted children who have lived and are living useful, productive, happy and normal lives. It has also become painfully apparent that many do not. It would appear that many adopted children run into problems and difficulties which often follow set patterns. This makes sense when one considers the background. Many children who are adopted have been born to single mothers – often teenage girls – to whom the mere fact of pregnancy was a disaster in itself. However much one feels for the single girl who finds herself in such a situation, the fact remains that the first 'vibes' that a developing foetus picks up are negative ones. He or she is no sooner alive than someone wishes they didn't exist.

One of the most common feelings among adopted young people is that of abandonment – rejection. As their maturity increases and they begin to understand, at least with the intellect, the reasons behind their situation, 'reason' may tell them one thing but 'feelings' tell them another. I had an instance recently. This family had two adopted daughters. The older one was beautiful, talented, and a well-adjusted teenager. The younger one was a beautiful, talented and very maladjusted teenager. Both had been 'chosen'. Both had received similar love and care. The younger one was at loggerheads with mother. She baited her, rebelled against her, was insolent, rude, lazy and dishonest.

I undertook to intercede for her and it came to me during prayers that she deeply resented being 'deserted, abandoned and given away'. She was angry with her natural mother and had transferred her resentment and anger to the adoptive mother. Of course it was unreasonable, but feelings triumph over reason every time. Reason tells us she should have been pleased and thankful towards her adoptive mother, but reason didn't even get to the starting line. Feelings again, were uppermost in this situation.

Many adopted young people are trying to fit into families in which they feel they don't belong, even though it is the only family they have ever known. Often it is not so much their natural parents they want to find. What they are really looking for are reasons why they are like they are. 'I wonder where I get my love of music from?' 'I wonder if my father was an athlete?' 'How come I've always loved animals so much?' 'Was my mother artistic – or good at languages, or mechanically inclined, or fond of gardening – or whatever?' Lack of knowledge about their roots seems to be at the bottom of a lot of their problems.

Somehow, although the young folk belong physically in their adoptive family, there are still the mysterious ties of generations to be considered and they seem to continue to be linked, in a way which we do not understand, to their own forebears. In most instances like this, when one prays for these young people, one must, in the name of Jesus, sever the link between the young person and the natural parents and then 're-bond' the young person to their adoptive family – mother, father and any other brothers and sisters.

Jesus is not only the great healer of people but He is also the great healer of relationships too.

If the family is Christian, re-bond to Jesus Himself. Just this simple act, done in faith, has made a transformed family unit out of a chaotic jumble. I know. I've watched it happen.

I have been asked about the whole issue of severing links, or breaking soul-ties as some folk describe it. We are talking about the tie between spirit and spirit. If we pray that any good link between natural parents and child remain intact and that anything detrimental be severed, we are acting with the child's long-term good in mind.

Another thing I always do is ask forgiveness for the natural parents. However much we know, understand and sympathise with them, the fact remains that by their actions they began a human life with little, if any, thought for that life. In fact, often their first thought towards that tiny spark was to stamp it out! Someone, somewhere, needs to express regret that we have, as a human race, treated our creative gift so casually, and that the result is seen as nothing but a nuisance, a disaster or a tragedy. This expression of regret, in prayer, is something that I always do. For the young person, I pray that any good thing which they have inherited from their ancestors will flourish and continue to grow but that anything harmful or detrimental will be cut off without trace.

Sometimes there are added complications. I remember one occasion when the lass concerned needed deliverance. She had formed the habit – when she was first told about her own adoption – of day-dreaming, romanticising and concocting all manner of make-believe stories and speculations about her origins. The more she allowed her mind to wander along these paths, the more difficult she found it to come back to reality. Her behaviour became quite bizarre. There was a single entity involved named 'fantasy'. I dismissed it myself. She said she'd had a strange dream. She'd dreamed that she was a child again and she held in her hand a bunch of brightly coloured balloons. In some eerie way the sky grew dark and her balloons ended up as so many round rocks, like cobblestones, about her feet. It was the dream which gave me the clue as to the name of the spirit. The 'dark' had come on the scene and changed the bright, happy, colourful things into concrete hard stumbling blocks. Her fantasies became impediments to her progress. Strange, wasn't it?

I believe I've written enough for today. It is such a vast and varied topic. I'm sure there are no two adopted children who think alike about their background, circumstances, parents – adoptive or natural – or themselves. We must listen to each one, hear them out, look behind their behaviour for the causes of it and pray for wisdom and commonsense. We need to intercede with sensitivity and compassion, assessing their needs as best we can.

I have only given you a few very broad outlines and you will have to fill in the gaps yourselves when the time comes. Nevertheless, what I have told you is sound and has been effective in many instances. Sometimes improvement has been immediate and rapid and at other times, prolonged and slow. At least you have some idea now, of what to look for and what to do next.

Letter 20

Dear Mark and Sarah

It is time, I'm sure, that I kept my promise to you to write about guidance – a vast and comprehensive topic upon which many folk much more capable than I have written extensively.

I had a friend who, at the time we're talking about, was a fairly new Christian without much church background and a very limited knowledge of the Bible. Her method of 'guidance' was that she would pray and then wait for God to drop an idea into her head. It worked very well for her until the day when someone she knew was in hospital. She prayed 'Lord, do you want me to go and see him or not? Please tell me.' Nothing happened. No bells rang. No lights flashed. No ideas dropped into her head. Silence. Very curious. God had always told her before – why not this time? What had she done wrong? Why was God not speaking? Did this silence indicate that she was not to go? She became unsettled and distressed and just a little desperate. Finally she prayed yet again 'Lord, why aren't you telling me what to do?' and into her mind crept the answer, as softly as the breeze in the trees. 'I already have.' That was all. Confusion reigned. She phoned a friend who was able to tell her the scripture in Matthew 25:35 & 36 which says that we are to feed the hungry, clothe the needy, care for the sick and visit prisoners and that *'anything that you did for one of my brothers here, however humble, you did for Me.'* God had indeed told her already.

We have the 'handbook', the 'tour guide', but the day to day travel plans may vary a little as we go, according to changes in conditions at the time. The time had come for her to grow up, read her own handbook and not expect to be told every tiny detail like a child. I have spoken about this topic of guidance to many people over the years and I usually tell them what someone once told me, 'Not even God can steer a stationary car!' When we begin to move, we get steered as we go and usually our opportunities for service and ministry come in the course of the day to day business of living. Some doors open, other doors shut, and we must be prepared to let it happen.

If we want to know every minute detail before we set out, it can hardly be called walking by faith. Of course there are exceptions – there always are. Sometimes we do get 'told' in detail, before we begin even, but what I'm saying is that such instances usually are just that – exceptions.

I have known many keen young people who, because they are reluctant to put a foot wrong, tend to sit tight and make no move at all, waiting for a 'nod or a prod from God'. In their enthusiasm, they expect an instant revelation. God, in His mercy, sometimes does settle our uncertainties in an unmistakable, memorable way, but I have actually heard people demand that God show them this or that. How easy it is to expect to walk by sight. We want to know everything.

Generally speaking, it would be true to say that anything purporting to be guidance from God which does not tie up with the principles laid down in scripture is highly suspect. To soak up scripture is a wonderful thing – it is our built-in safeguard against mistakes. So how **do** we hear the voice of God apart from the written word? The Bible tells us of many ways.

Samuel, Peter and Saul – later Paul – and Philip, all heard audible voices. Then there was the 'collective and silent impression' – *'It seemed good to the Holy Spirit and to us'*

(Acts 15:28). On other occasions messengers were sent. Lot was warned of approaching disaster, Peter was led out of jail. Both Joseph and the wise men had dreams and they followed those 'dream instructions'. The Old Testament is full of the voices of the prophets saying 'If this – then that', but even with their warnings, people still chose the wrong way. Peter had his vision of the animals while he was up on the roof and Paul had his dream/vision about the man from Macedonia. There were, at times, sets of positive circumstances, such as led to Paul's meeting with Lydia at Philippi, and sets of negative ones as he discovered when he wanted to preach in Asia but found the Holy Spirit diverting him elsewhere as doors around him refused to open.

The list is endless. Search for yourselves. We are all human. We sometimes hear only what we want to hear. At other times we hear but misinterpret, or, having heard we choose to disregard. Also, being human, we can sometimes be deceived. It would appear that God leads, prompts and encourages, and although at times, we feel a sense of urgency about some course of action, yet God does not compel or force. There is an old saying 'God leads – the devil drives' which we do well to remember.

A friend once told me about a situation in a church she knew about. A young couple were expecting their first baby. The mother was 'told' in a vision that her child would be a boy – to be called John – a second John the Baptist who would herald the Lord's return to earth. She was 'ordered' by a 'shining presence' to tell everyone and she and her young husband did. She felt 'compelled' and was unhappy when she was not 'telling'. Some believed her. Others did not.

At last the child was born – a beautiful little girl. The mother was stunned. She rejected the child. She had a breakdown. The husband was distraught. The young mother's family were divided by doubt and argument. The young couple lost their faith and their church was split down the middle. What had gone wrong?

They were so caught up with the thrill of the vision that they failed to recognise that God may not have sent it. She had felt 'compelled' to tell. She was driven!

John Wesley said:

> 'Do not hastily ascribe all things to God. Do not too easily suppose dreams, voices, impressions, or revelations to be from God. They **may** be from Him, they may be from nature, they may be from the devil. Therefore believe not every spirit but try (test) the spirits, whether they be of God' (1 John 4:1).

Two ways in which we can test are to ask God for confirmation, and to check with someone else. If the young mother-to-be had consulted her pastor before she spread her story, he could perhaps have pointed out what she and her husband missed – the possibility of harm and division. Her vision had its origin in 'nature' and her grand hopes for her child, which were in turn used by the opposition to urge her into rash and unthinking behaviour which brought chaos to so many.

Another mother whom I know, had a most unsettling and disturbing dream. She dreamt – among other things – that her elder daughter was destined for an early death. She couldn't get it out of her mind. She phoned the minister for an appointment and she phoned me and asked me to pray. Into my mind came the words of John 10:10 *'The thief came to steal and kill and destroy.'* Here was refreshing sleep being stolen and peace of mind being destroyed. I phoned the minister and told him that I knew what was at the bottom of her troubles. A spirit was afflicting her and its name was 'false prophecy'. The whole dream was a tissue of lies.

He ministered to her, her fears left and she never had the dream again. The daughter is still alive and well.

What about voices? I had what I call a 'Cornelius experience' myself once. I was heading towards the shops one day and a voice in my ear said 'Go to Ruth's place.'

I replied 'But Lord, I've got to do the shopping this morning.' Nevertheless I went to Ruth's place. She had a puzzle or two which she couldn't seem to work through and had prayed, 'Lord, send me someone who can explain it to me.' I had got 'sent'. We had a wonderful morning which neither of us has ever forgotten.

I must tell you though, about another voice and another dream. A friend phoned and asked if I would pray for her husband who was to undergo heart surgery. I promised. About 4 o'clock on the morning of his impending operation I dreamt that he died under the anaesthetic. Was I being warned? How do you pray in faith with that size dollop of doubt lurking? The Bible says *'Pray for one another that you might be healed'* and my dream was saying I shouldn't pray for his recovery as he was going to die. Which was the truth?

A 'voice' told me to go to my minister and ask for prayers for myself. Then another voice said 'You'll do no such thing!' He had also been asked to pray for the man concerned. If I were to go and unload my doubts into the minister's ears maybe he would have doubts too. Then there would be two doubtful people instead of one, and half the amount of faith being exercised on the patient's behalf. So I sat on it and told nobody until the surgery was safely over and done with. I recognised the opposition at work. We are told to encourage one another in our faith, not discourage one another with our doubts!

There was more to do yet. It was not enough to passively resist. We need to go a step further and counteract. I got the concordance and looked up many verses with 'life' in them, committed a few to memory and repeated them, in my mind, all morning. The patient is still with us.

Do you see what happened? The dream arose from nature. My **mind** was aware of the risks and dangers so the dream was used to plant doubt and I nearly passed it on. Which voice does one listen to in instances like this? The one which leads to a scripture, such as, for instance,

'Let everything be done for the building up of the saints' – not for the dragging down of the same.

If anyone you know has a dream/vision/voice involving calamity or destruction, be careful how it is discussed. It may be a genuine warning, in which case you may be alerted to take evasive action – as I wrote about in my letter on dreams – and to pray in faith that tragedy may be avoided. This is what I did. I resisted the negative and asserted the opposite.

We have covered a great deal about guidance but a few points still need to be mentioned. The scriptures are our handbook, so we begin walking in obedience and we are steered as we go. Does where you want to go line up with the handbook? Do you have an inner conviction of the rightness of it? If in doubt, have you cross-checked? Lastly, is your timing right? Maturity does have certain advantages in these matters. There is a lot to be learned by trial and error. We tend to rely less on human reasoning and feelings, and more on faith and the known nature of God. God is gentle while we learn. We are like children struggling to walk. We're encouraged when we manage it and are comforted if we crash. The aim is to be upright and well coordinated and a few struggles and crashes seem to be part of the learning process. It is not a tragedy if we put a foot wrong. The real tragedy is the failure to walk at all.

I'm sure we can all spot the danger of lifting isolated verses out of context and yet, let's face it, in times of stress we have all done it and the marvel of it all is that God, in His mercy, knowing our distress, often does speak to us through such a questionable procedure. Who said the days of miracles are over?

Letter 21

Dear Mark and Sarah

The next two topics which you ask about are 'love' and 'forgiveness' but they will have to wait. I simply must tell you a wonderful story. These things happened to a friend of a friend of mine, whom I saw by chance the other day. I asked her how her new job was working out and she proceeded to tell me.

It transpired that she, an attractive lady who is a very competent typist had always had what she called a 'person problem'. It reared its head every time she had anything to do with intellectual people. Circumstances would arise in which she would find a rising resentment within herself saying 'Who does he think he is?' this attitude had led to her failure to stick with several good jobs, as the increasingly antagonistic atmosphere made it impossible for her to work constructively. As her new boss was also a dyed-in-the-wool academic, she could see trouble ahead. She was at a stage in life when, because of several exciting things which had happened to members of her family and people around her, she was progressing spiritually, in leaps and bounds.

There came a day when she prayed, 'Lord, I don't want to go through it all over again. It's time I got it right. Show me how.'

And He did! 'It was like a TV screen,' she related. 'I saw

myself in school in Year Two, sitting at a desk in the classroom, wearing a dunce's hat. I've been wearing it all these years.'

Of course she's not a dunce. She's a highly intelligent lady but she struggled, at school, because she didn't fit into the prescribed mould. The teacher had obviously employed the tactics in order to jolt her into making a greater effort. The little girl who was humiliated in front of others, presumably smarter than she was, had become the adult woman who was still feeling the old feelings, and who floundered out of her depth when in close contact with the 'clever' ones of this world.

'I hope no teacher these days uses such tactics with a child,' I exploded. 'It makes me annoyed when I hear something like that. Here you are, struggling with it for years.'

'I saw the teacher,' she said. 'The teacher was crying and I said "it's all right now. Don't cry any more. I've forgiven you." '

'I hope you've got rid of your hat now,' I said. 'I wrecked it,' she replied. 'I cut it up with the scissors. The whole thing was incredible. I said to Jesus, "I haven't got my hat on any more, have I?" He said, "No, I've got your hat on now"   and I looked and He did have my hat – but there were thorns on His head and He was bleeding.'

We both choked back our tears and swallowed the lump in our throats. It was a moving moment. 'I just know,' she said, 'that Jesus took my dunce's cap with Him to the Cross and there is no way I'm ever going to wear it again.'

I knew you'd appreciate this story. I've tried to remember it exactly as she told it to me.

Letter 22

Dear Mark and Sarah

Now to get down to work with what you wanted to know. You refer to an occasion when I once used a quote from Huxley about loving people. 'They are detestable because we detest them. If we loved them, they would be lovable.' You are puzzled, I take note, by the way in which we feel guilty because there are some people whom we just can't feel loving towards.

Let me tell you a story. At one time I worked as a nurse aide in a private hospital, and during the college holidays the matron would sometimes employ teenagers who were considering a career in nursing, both to help the regular staff, and to give the girls a trial run at the job.

One such lass worked with me on my afternoon duty and if anyone was ideally suited to the profession, she was. Not only was she capable, she was also caring, and seemed to have an inexhaustible supply of patience with the patients, and a degree of maturity beyond her years.

There came a day however, when I discovered her in the sluice room, with the taps turned full on full bore in order to disguise the sound of her sobs. I asked her what the matter was.

'I'll never make a nurse,' she wept, 'if old Granny Whatnot spits her dinner down my clean smock once more, I'll scream! Don't you see – I can't love them.'

I quickly sent a prayer heavenwards, and then suddenly I knew what to say.

'Now listen to me,' I said in my best reproving tone, 'I don't want to hear another word of this nonsense. Don't you see – you **are** loving them?'

'How do you mean?' she asked.

'Well, I continued, 'you think about the Good Samaritan in the Bible. He's gone down in history as a first-class example of a truly loving man. Now you can't tell me he felt all slushy and sentimental about that dirty, beat-up guy lying in the roadway. He was probably thinking what a mess he was and wondering if the bandits would jump out from behind the rocks and have a go at him! The main thing is – what did he do? He was basically a compassionate man. The story says that he was moved by compassion. That was his underlying motivation whatever his surface feelings may have been. He did the decent, civilised thing. He did more than anybody else – at considerable cost to himself. All the others had hurried away. He made plans for the man's long-term care. Don't you see? We aren't told how he felt, only what he decided to do, and he is considered to be a fine example of a truly loving man.'

'Do you mean,' she said, 'that it's what I do that counts and not just how I feel?'

'Yes,' I replied, 'I mean just that. Mind you, if you **do** feel good towards them that makes it easier to decide, but as you said yourself, sometimes the good feelings are not there, but so what? We decide anyway. You are going to be a first-class nurse, working for the long-term good of helpless people. That, young lady, is love in action whether you feel sentimental about people or not.'

This point is one that many people never grasp. It's what we decide to do that counts. Now I'm not saying that there is no place for sentiment or deep feeling. Our word 'love' is made to serve too many purposes. The Greeks had the right idea. They had many different words for many kinds of love – love of country, love of family, love of husband or wife and many others.

There is ample scope for deep feeling but it should not be only what we feel that motivates us but rather obedience to the 'law of love' which says in effect, to 'act always for the ultimate well-being of whoever it is'. Sometimes it is not only obedience which motivates us. The obedience itself has a deeper motive – it is that of compassion. So feelings often do come into the picture. Jesus Himself was moved with compassion to attend to the hordes of sick people whom He encountered. Compassion and action go hand in hand.

Many people do not act for the long-term good of others. Our society is riddled with crime, deceit and violence of once kind or another. We have, collectively speaking, disobeyed the law of love and we are all suffering the consequences. It is a strange thing, but when we do decide to act in a loving manner, even if we don't feel particularly loving, our feelings often undergo a subtle change – particularly if we also decide to pray for the person concerned. We find that they don't rile us quite as much as they used to. They might even have a few good points hidden away!

This brings us to the other topic which you asked me to write about – that of forgiveness. Most of us, if we've been badly hurt, find it difficult to forgive and yet, if we don't learn how we are in deep trouble.

I remember once being at a meeting once and the speaker made a statement. He was trying to emphasise the forgiving nature of God and he said, 'God's forgiveness is like God's love – it's unconditional.' Don't you believe it! I had to go and speak to him afterwards. Matthew 6:14 & 15 reads,

> *'For if you forgive others the wrongs they have done, your heavenly Father will also forgive you – but if you do not forgive others, then the wrongs you have done will not be forgiven by your Father.'*

If that isn't conditional, what is?

The poor startled speaker did not expect to be pulled up by a crazy lady waving her Bible at him, but he realised that what he had meant to say had not come out right and he took steps to remedy the situation. He was trying to say that God loves people not because they deserve it but because it is His nature to love. Likewise He forgives people not because they've earned it but because it is His nature to forgive.

His forgiveness does not become operative in our lives until we appropriate it and we can't appropriate it with any degree of understanding until we become aware of what it costs. In other words, until we forgive other people and allow relationships to be restored, we haven't the remotest idea of what it cost God to forgive us.

This isn't complicated – just very profound. It is when we regret what we have done and what we have failed to do, that the forgiveness of God becomes real. An 'unrepentant sinner' often has no idea of the extent of his own estrangement. There's that word 'sin' again. Many people's notion of forgiveness is that God, or anybody else for that matter, turns a blind eye to their misdoings, lets them off the hook or condones what they are doing, and so life goes on much the same. We all need to be reminded that God does not condone sin – He forgives it. One costs nothing. The other costs everything. Jesus, on the Cross, prayed for forgiveness for those who were causing His death! What an example to follow.

Sometimes you will meet people who, because they want to have a bit of a moan (legitimate or otherwise), will tell you what you have said or done to upset them – but that they forgive you. This kind of remark usually sound patronising in the extreme and causes most people's hackles to rise. There are other ways of saying what needs to be said.

We talk a great deal about healing and wholeness but I venture to say that being able to forgive those who wrong us and being able to forgive ourselves for the wrongs we have done to others, are two of the most important factors in the 'making whole' of people. Whichever way we look at it, it's costly. To forgive is to ensure that a fractured relationship is restored. We lay aside our right to be angry. In some instances we have every right to be angry or resentful but if we continue to be that way, we are in the process of becoming angry and resentful people. Better to let it go than to live on in bitterness.

This means that forgiveness is also a decision, and not necessarily only a feeling. Initially we may not feel very forgiving but if we persist in our decision the feelings eventually do change. One friend told me that when she came up against a brick wall, she begins to live as though the whole thing were already resolved. This is love in action. This is forgiveness in action. It requires imagination. It requires decision. It requires determination but it is a reliable recipe for a changed life.

That's all for now.
With love

Beryl